JEOPARDY! ™

What Is Quiz Book 3?

Other Books

Jeopardy! . . . What Is Quiz Book 1?

Jeopardy! . . . What Is Quiz Book 2?

Jeopardy! . . . What Is Quiz Book 4?

JEOPARDY!™

What Is Quiz Book 3?

**Andrews McMeel
Publishing**

Kansas City

Book design by Holly Camerlinck

Composition by Kelly & Company,
Lee's Summit, Missouri

ISBN: 0-7407-1214-4

JEOPARDY!™

What Is Quiz Book 3?

**Andrews McMeel
Publishing**

Kansas City

JEOPARDY!

FOOD & DRINK

BY DEFINITION, A SANDWICH THAT IS OPEN-FACED LACKS THIS ON TOP	$100	WHAT IS
THIS BASIC SAUCE NAMED FOR ITS COLOR IS OFTEN THE FOUNDATION OF CHEESE SAUCE	$200	WHAT IS
OFTEN SERVED WITH FRUIT FOR DESSERT, TALEGGIO IS A CHEESE FROM THIS COUNTRY	$300	WHAT IS
YOU CAN ADD A DE-LIGHTFULLY WOODSY FLAVOR TO YOUR ENTREES WITH PORCINI, A TYPE OF THESE	$400	WHAT ARE
"FORMOSA" OFTEN PRECEDES THE NAME OF THIS TEA WHOSE NAME COMES FROM THE CHINESE FOR "BLACK DRAGON"	$500	WHAT IS

JEOPARDY!

FOOD & DRINK

$100   WHAT IS BREAD? $100

$200   WHAT IS WHITE SAUCE? $200

$300   WHAT IS ITALY? $300

$400   WHAT ARE MUSHROOMS? $400

$500   WHAT IS OOLONG? $500

JEOPARDY!™

BIOGRAPHIES

MERLE MILLER'S 1980 BOOK "LYNDON" IS "AN ORAL BIOGRAPHY" OF THIS MAN	**$100**	WHO IS
A 1991 BOOK ABOUT THIS ACTOR, JFK'S BROTHER-IN-LAW, IS SUBTITLED "THE MAN WHO KEPT THE SECRETS"	**$200**	WHO IS
LOUIS HARLAN'S BIOGRAPHY OF THIS TUSKEGEE EDUCATOR WON A 1984 PULITZER PRIZE	**$300**	WHO IS
THE TABLES WERE TURNED ON THIS BIOGRAPHER WHEN SHE BECAME THE SUBJECT OF THE UNAUTHORIZED BOOK "POISON PEN"	**$400**	WHO IS
"THE MAN WHO PRESUMED" TELLS THE STORY OF THIS EXPLORER	**$500**	WHO IS

JEOPARDY!

BIOGRAPHIES

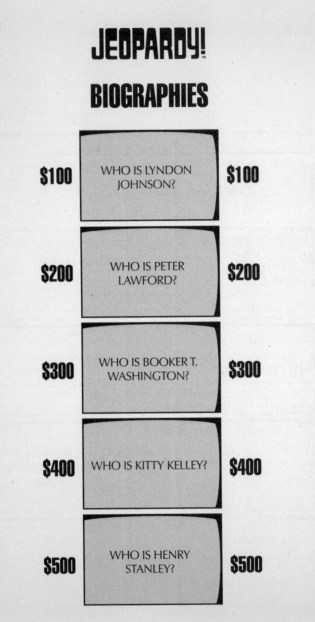

$100 — WHO IS LYNDON JOHNSON? — $100

$200 — WHO IS PETER LAWFORD? — $200

$300 — WHO IS BOOKER T. WASHINGTON? — $300

$400 — WHO IS KITTY KELLEY? — $400

$500 — WHO IS HENRY STANLEY? — $500

4

JEOPARDY!

THE MOVIES

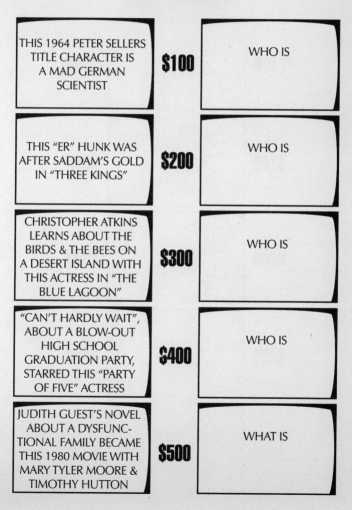

THIS 1964 PETER SELLERS TITLE CHARACTER IS A MAD GERMAN SCIENTIST	$100	WHO IS
THIS "ER" HUNK WAS AFTER SADDAM'S GOLD IN "THREE KINGS"	$200	WHO IS
CHRISTOPHER ATKINS LEARNS ABOUT THE BIRDS & THE BEES ON A DESERT ISLAND WITH THIS ACTRESS IN "THE BLUE LAGOON"	$300	WHO IS
"CAN'T HARDLY WAIT", ABOUT A BLOW-OUT HIGH SCHOOL GRADUATION PARTY, STARRED THIS "PARTY OF FIVE" ACTRESS	$400	WHO IS
JUDITH GUEST'S NOVEL ABOUT A DYSFUNC-TIONAL FAMILY BECAME THIS 1980 MOVIE WITH MARY TYLER MOORE & TIMOTHY HUTTON	$500	WHAT IS

JEOPARDY!

THE MOVIES

$100   WHO IS DR. STRANGELOVE? $100

$200   WHO IS GEORGE CLOONEY? $200

$300   WHO IS BROOKE SHIELDS? $300

$400   WHO IS JENNIFER LOVE HEWITT? $400

$500   WHAT IS "ORDINARY PEOPLE"? $500

JEOPARDY!

AMERICAN HISTORY

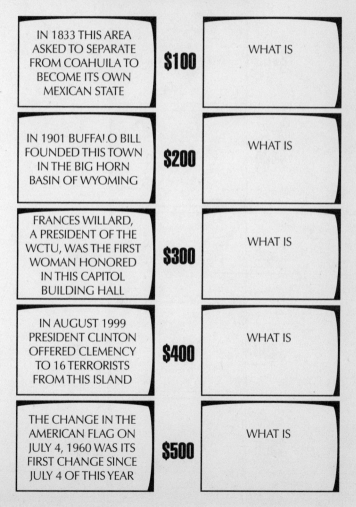

IN 1833 THIS AREA ASKED TO SEPARATE FROM COAHUILA TO BECOME ITS OWN MEXICAN STATE	$100	WHAT IS
IN 1901 BUFFALO BILL FOUNDED THIS TOWN IN THE BIG HORN BASIN OF WYOMING	$200	WHAT IS
FRANCES WILLARD, A PRESIDENT OF THE WCTU, WAS THE FIRST WOMAN HONORED IN THIS CAPITOL BUILDING HALL	$300	WHAT IS
IN AUGUST 1999 PRESIDENT CLINTON OFFERED CLEMENCY TO 16 TERRORISTS FROM THIS ISLAND	$400	WHAT IS
THE CHANGE IN THE AMERICAN FLAG ON JULY 4, 1960 WAS ITS FIRST CHANGE SINCE JULY 4 OF THIS YEAR	$500	WHAT IS

JEOPARDY!™

AMERICAN HISTORY

$100   WHAT IS TEXAS? $100

$200   WHAT IS CODY? $200

$300   WHAT IS (NATIONAL) STATUARY HALL? $300

$400   WHAT IS PUERTO RICO? $400

$500   WHAT IS 1959? $500

JEOPARDY!

NUTRITION

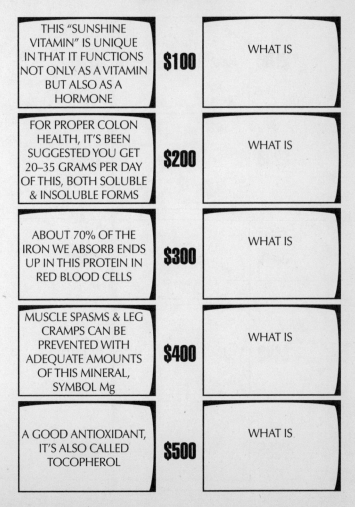

Clue	Value	Response
THIS "SUNSHINE VITAMIN" IS UNIQUE IN THAT IT FUNCTIONS NOT ONLY AS A VITAMIN BUT ALSO AS A HORMONE	$100	WHAT IS
FOR PROPER COLON HEALTH, IT'S BEEN SUGGESTED YOU GET 20–35 GRAMS PER DAY OF THIS, BOTH SOLUBLE & INSOLUBLE FORMS	$200	WHAT IS
ABOUT 70% OF THE IRON WE ABSORB ENDS UP IN THIS PROTEIN IN RED BLOOD CELLS	$300	WHAT IS
MUSCLE SPASMS & LEG CRAMPS CAN BE PREVENTED WITH ADEQUATE AMOUNTS OF THIS MINERAL, SYMBOL Mg	$400	WHAT IS
A GOOD ANTIOXIDANT, IT'S ALSO CALLED TOCOPHEROL	$500	WHAT IS

JEOPARDY!

NUTRITION

$100 WHAT IS VITAMIN D? **$100**

$200 WHAT IS FIBER? **$200**

$300 WHAT IS THE HEMOGLOBIN? **$300**

$400 WHAT IS MAGNESIUM? **$400**

$500 WHAT IS VITAMIN E? **$500**

JEOPARDY!

THE "IN" SOUND

THE SOUTH AMERICAN EMPIRE OF THESE PEOPLE INCLUDED PARTS OF PRESENT-DAY ECUADOR, PERU, CHILE & ARGENTINA	**$100**	WHO ARE
FROM THE LATIN FOR "TO SET ON FIRE", IT'S AN AROMATIC SUBSTANCE BURNED TO PRODUCE A PLEASANT ODOR	**$200**	WHAT IS
THE MAIN ISLANDS OF THIS COUNTRY INCLUDE BORNEO, SULAWESI, JAVA & SUMATRA	**$300**	WHAT IS
USUALLY THE LARGEST BRANCH OF AN ARMY, IT'S ANOTHER NAME FOR FOOT SOLDIERS	**$400**	WHAT IS
A FURNACE-LIKE DEVICE FOR REDUCING WASTE PRODUCTS TO ASH	**$500**	WHAT IS

JEOPARDY!

THE "IN" SOUND

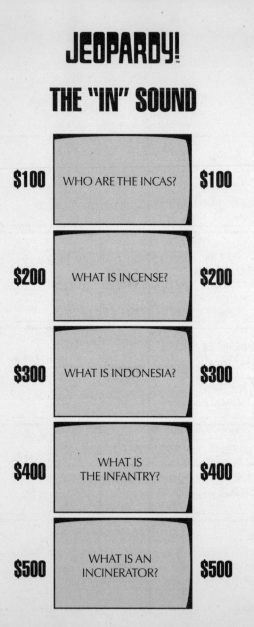

$100   WHO ARE THE INCAS? $100

$200   WHAT IS INCENSE? $200

$300   WHAT IS INDONESIA? $300

$400   WHAT IS THE INFANTRY? $400

$500   WHAT IS AN INCINERATOR? $500

12

DOUBLE JEOPARDY!

ISLAND COUNTRIES

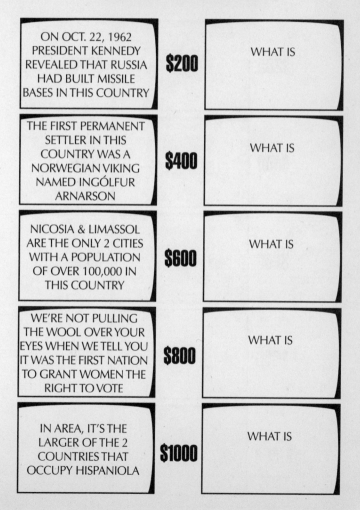

ON OCT. 22, 1962 PRESIDENT KENNEDY REVEALED THAT RUSSIA HAD BUILT MISSILE BASES IN THIS COUNTRY	$200	WHAT IS
THE FIRST PERMANENT SETTLER IN THIS COUNTRY WAS A NORWEGIAN VIKING NAMED INGÓLFUR ARNARSON	$400	WHAT IS
NICOSIA & LIMASSOL ARE THE ONLY 2 CITIES WITH A POPULATION OF OVER 100,000 IN THIS COUNTRY	$600	WHAT IS
WE'RE NOT PULLING THE WOOL OVER YOUR EYES WHEN WE TELL YOU IT WAS THE FIRST NATION TO GRANT WOMEN THE RIGHT TO VOTE	$800	WHAT IS
IN AREA, IT'S THE LARGER OF THE 2 COUNTRIES THAT OCCUPY HISPANIOLA	$1000	WHAT IS

DOUBLE JEOPARDY!

ISLAND COUNTRIES

$200	WHAT IS CUBA?	$200
$400	WHAT IS ICELAND?	$400
$600	WHAT IS CYPRUS?	$600
$800	WHAT IS NEW ZEALAND?	$800
$1000	WHAT IS THE DOMINICAN REPUBLIC?	$1000

14

DOUBLE JEOPARDY!

5-LETTER WORDS

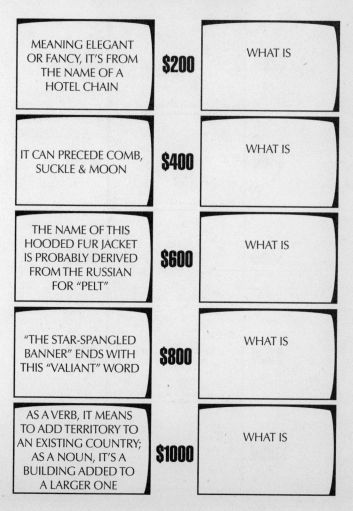

MEANING ELEGANT OR FANCY, IT'S FROM THE NAME OF A HOTEL CHAIN	$200	WHAT IS
IT CAN PRECEDE COMB, SUCKLE & MOON	$400	WHAT IS
THE NAME OF THIS HOODED FUR JACKET IS PROBABLY DERIVED FROM THE RUSSIAN FOR "PELT"	$600	WHAT IS
"THE STAR-SPANGLED BANNER" ENDS WITH THIS "VALIANT" WORD	$800	WHAT IS
AS A VERB, IT MEANS TO ADD TERRITORY TO AN EXISTING COUNTRY; AS A NOUN, IT'S A BUILDING ADDED TO A LARGER ONE	$1000	WHAT IS

DOUBLE JEOPARDY!

5-LETTER WORDS

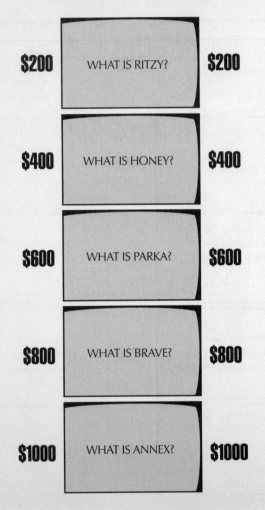

$200   WHAT IS RITZY? $200

$400   WHAT IS HONEY? $400

$600   WHAT IS PARKA? $600

$800   WHAT IS BRAVE? $800

$1000   WHAT IS ANNEX? $1000

DOUBLE JEOPARDY!

LADIES OF LITERATURE

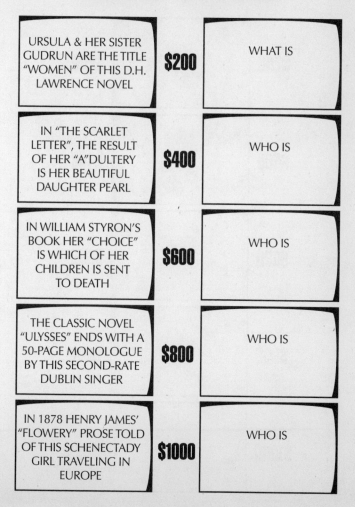

URSULA & HER SISTER GUDRUN ARE THE TITLE "WOMEN" OF THIS D.H. LAWRENCE NOVEL	**$200**	WHAT IS
IN "THE SCARLET LETTER", THE RESULT OF HER "A"DULTERY IS HER BEAUTIFUL DAUGHTER PEARL	**$400**	WHO IS
IN WILLIAM STYRON'S BOOK HER "CHOICE" IS WHICH OF HER CHILDREN IS SENT TO DEATH	**$600**	WHO IS
THE CLASSIC NOVEL "ULYSSES" ENDS WITH A 50-PAGE MONOLOGUE BY THIS SECOND-RATE DUBLIN SINGER	**$800**	WHO IS
IN 1878 HENRY JAMES' "FLOWERY" PROSE TOLD OF THIS SCHENECTADY GIRL TRAVELING IN EUROPE	**$1000**	WHO IS

DOUBLE JEOPARDY!

LADIES OF LITERATURE

$200   WHAT IS "WOMEN IN LOVE"? $200

$400   WHO IS HESTER PRYNNE? $400

$600   WHO IS SOPHIE (ZAWISTOWSKA)? $600

$800   WHO IS MOLLY BLOOM? $800

$1000   WHO IS DAISY MILLER? $1000

DOUBLE JEOPARDY!

YOU AUTO KNOW

SQUEEZE THESE RADI-ATOR ATTACHMENTS & REPLACE THEM IF THEY'RE GOING SOFT ON YOU	**$200**	WHAT ARE
THE ONE USED TO CHECK POWER STEERING FLUID IS SHORTER THAN THE ONE USED TO CHECK ENGINE OIL	**$400**	WHAT IS
LIKE A COMEDIAN, A CAR OWNER MAY NEED TO "ADJUST" THIS, PER-HAPS BY ADVANCING THE SPARK	**$600**	WHAT IS
ALSO THE NAME OF A COMIC STRIP, IT MAKES THE PISTONS' UP-&-DOWN MOTION CIRCULAR	**$800**	WHAT IS
THROTTLE-BODY & MULTIPORT ARE THE 2 MAIN TYPES OF THIS SYSTEM OF DELIVERING GAS TO THE ENGINE	**$1000**	WHAT IS

DOUBLE JEOPARDY!

YOU AUTO KNOW

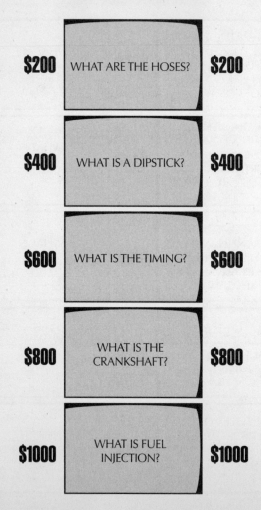

$200	WHAT ARE THE HOSES?	**$200**
$400	WHAT IS A DIPSTICK?	**$400**
$600	WHAT IS THE TIMING?	**$600**
$800	WHAT IS THE CRANKSHAFT?	**$800**
$1000	WHAT IS FUEL INJECTION?	**$1000**

DOUBLE JEOPARDY!

1960s POP MUSIC

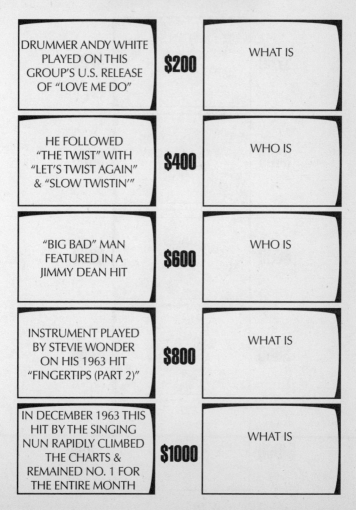

DRUMMER ANDY WHITE PLAYED ON THIS GROUP'S U.S. RELEASE OF "LOVE ME DO"	$200	WHAT IS
HE FOLLOWED "THE TWIST" WITH "LET'S TWIST AGAIN" & "SLOW TWISTIN'"	$400	WHO IS
"BIG BAD" MAN FEATURED IN A JIMMY DEAN HIT	$600	WHO IS
INSTRUMENT PLAYED BY STEVIE WONDER ON HIS 1963 HIT "FINGERTIPS (PART 2)"	$800	WHAT IS
IN DECEMBER 1963 THIS HIT BY THE SINGING NUN RAPIDLY CLIMBED THE CHARTS & REMAINED NO. 1 FOR THE ENTIRE MONTH	$1000	WHAT IS

DOUBLE JEOPARDY!

1960s POP MUSIC

$200

WHAT IS
THE BEATLES?

$200

$400

WHO IS CHUBBY
CHECKER?

$400

$600

WHO IS "BIG BAD
JOHN"?

$600

$800

WHAT IS THE
HARMONICA?

$800

$1000

WHAT IS
"DOMINIQUE"?

$1000

DOUBLE JEOPARDY!

THE CORNER DRUGSTORE

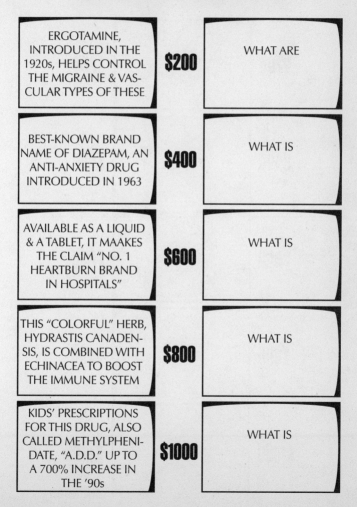

ERGOTAMINE, INTRODUCED IN THE 1920s, HELPS CONTROL THE MIGRAINE & VASCULAR TYPES OF THESE	**$200**	WHAT ARE
BEST-KNOWN BRAND NAME OF DIAZEPAM, AN ANTI-ANXIETY DRUG INTRODUCED IN 1963	**$400**	WHAT IS
AVAILABLE AS A LIQUID & A TABLET, IT MAAKES THE CLAIM "NO. 1 HEARTBURN BRAND IN HOSPITALS"	**$600**	WHAT IS
THIS "COLORFUL" HERB, HYDRASTIS CANADENSIS, IS COMBINED WITH ECHINACEA TO BOOST THE IMMUNE SYSTEM	**$800**	WHAT IS
KIDS' PRESCRIPTIONS FOR THIS DRUG, ALSO CALLED METHYLPHENIDATE, "A.D.D." UP TO A 700% INCREASE IN THE '90s	**$1000**	WHAT IS

DOUBLE JEOPARDY!

THE CORNER DRUGSTORE

$200 WHAT ARE HEADACHES? **$200**

$400 WHAT IS VALIUM? **$400**

$600 WHAT IS MAALOX? **$600**

$800 WHAT IS GOLDENSEAL? **$800**

$1000 WHAT IS RITALIN? **$1000**

24

FINAL JEOPARDY!

20th CENTURY LEADERS

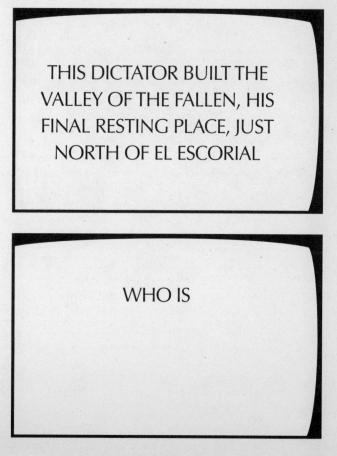

THIS DICTATOR BUILT THE
VALLEY OF THE FALLEN, HIS
FINAL RESTING PLACE, JUST
NORTH OF EL ESCORIAL

WHO IS

FINAL JEOPARDY!
20th CENTURY LEADERS

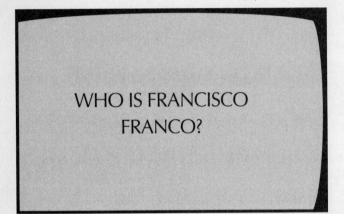

WHO IS FRANCISCO FRANCO?

JEOPARDY!

HISTORIC AMOURS

WHEN THIS "OLIVER TWIST" AUTHOR FELL FOR AN ACTRESS HIS WIFE TWISTED HIS ARM FOR A LEGAL SEPARATION	**$100**	WHO IS
HE PREFERRED THE "BOUNTY"OUS BEAUTY OF MAUATUA TO BLIGH & BREADFRUIT	**$200**	WHO IS
IT'S LIKELY THAT ETTA PLACE, THE COMPANION OF THIS "KID", WAS A LADY OF THE EVENING RATHER THAN A SCHOOLMARM	**$300**	WHO IS
ACTRESS NELL GWYN WAS THE LOVER OF LORD BUCKHURST BEFORE SHE CAUGHT THE EYE OF THIS "MERRY MONARCH"	**$400**	WHO IS
LOUIS I's LUST FOR LOLA MONTEZ LED HIM TO LOSE THE THRONE OF THIS GERMAN KINGDOM	**$500**	WHAT IS

JEOPARDY!

HISTORIC AMOURS

$100   WHO IS CHARLES DICKENS? $100

$200   WHO IS FLETCHER CHRISTIAN? $200

$300   WHO IS THE SUNDANCE KID? $300

$400   WHO IS CHARLES II? $400

$500   WHAT IS BAVARIA? $500

JEOPARDY!

U.S. GEOGRAPHY

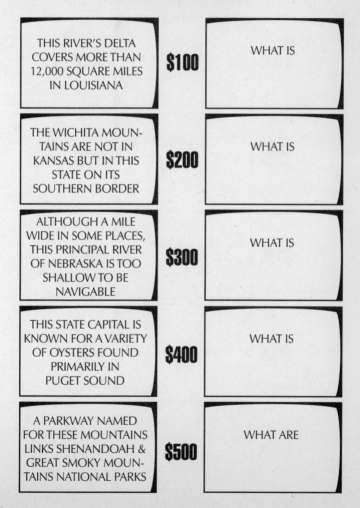

THIS RIVER'S DELTA COVERS MORE THAN 12,000 SQUARE MILES IN LOUISIANA	$100	WHAT IS
THE WICHITA MOUNTAINS ARE NOT IN KANSAS BUT IN THIS STATE ON ITS SOUTHERN BORDER	$200	WHAT IS
ALTHOUGH A MILE WIDE IN SOME PLACES, THIS PRINCIPAL RIVER OF NEBRASKA IS TOO SHALLOW TO BE NAVIGABLE	$300	WHAT IS
THIS STATE CAPITAL IS KNOWN FOR A VARIETY OF OYSTERS FOUND PRIMARILY IN PUGET SOUND	$400	WHAT IS
A PARKWAY NAMED FOR THESE MOUNTAINS LINKS SHENANDOAH & GREAT SMOKY MOUNTAINS NATIONAL PARKS	$500	WHAT ARE

29

JEOPARDY!

U.S. GEOGRAPHY

$100 — WHAT IS THE MISSISSIPPI RIVER? — $100

$200 — WHAT IS OKLAHOMA? — $200

$300 — WHAT IS THE PLATTE RIVER? — $300

$400 — WHAT IS OLYMPIA? — $400

$500 — WHAT ARE THE BLUE RIDGE MOUNTAINS? — $500

JEOPARDY!

SITCOMS

ON THIS SITCOM IN 1998, TIM TAYLOR'S SON RANDY RAN OFF TO WORK IN A COSTA RICAN RAINFOREST	**$100**	WHAT IS
ON HER SELF-TITLED SITCOM, SHE WORKED AT A PLASTICS FACTORY & A BEAUTY SALON BEFORE OPENING HER OWN DINER	**$200**	WHO IS
ENRICO COLANTONI PLAYS A PHOTOGRA-PHER & LAURA SAN GIACOMO A JOURN-ALIST ON THIS SHOW	**$300**	WHAT IS
ON THE WB SHOW NAMED FOR THIS COMIC, HE LIVES AT HIS FAMILY'S HOTEL WHILE STRIVING FOR STARDOM	**$400**	WHO IS
HER FIRST PRIMETIME ROLE WAS ON "KATE & ALLIE"; NOW SHE PLAYS KATE ON THE "THE DREW CAREY SHOW"	**$500**	WHO IS

JEOPARDY!

SITCOMS

$100 — WHAT IS "HOME IMPROVEMENT"? — $100

$200 — WHO IS ROSEANNE? — $200

$300 — WHAT IS "JUST SHOOT ME"? — $300

$400 — WHO IS JAMIE FOXX? — $400

$500 — WHO IS CHRISTA MILLER? — $500

JEOPARDY!™

TECHNOLOGY

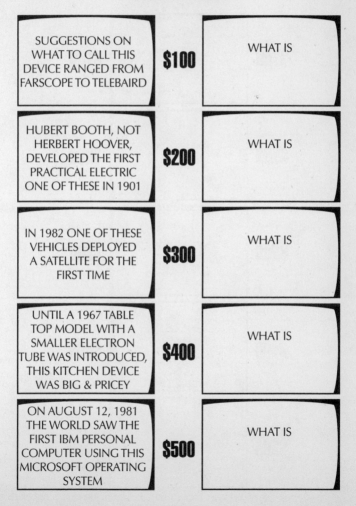

SUGGESTIONS ON WHAT TO CALL THIS DEVICE RANGED FROM FARSCOPE TO TELEBAIRD	**$100**	WHAT IS
HUBERT BOOTH, NOT HERBERT HOOVER, DEVELOPED THE FIRST PRACTICAL ELECTRIC ONE OF THESE IN 1901	**$200**	WHAT IS
IN 1982 ONE OF THESE VEHICLES DEPLOYED A SATELLITE FOR THE FIRST TIME	**$300**	WHAT IS
UNTIL A 1967 TABLE TOP MODEL WITH A SMALLER ELECTRON TUBE WAS INTRODUCED, THIS KITCHEN DEVICE WAS BIG & PRICEY	**$400**	WHAT IS
ON AUGUST 12, 1981 THE WORLD SAW THE FIRST IBM PERSONAL COMPUTER USING THIS MICROSOFT OPERATING SYSTEM	**$500**	WHAT IS

JEOPARDY!

TECHNOLOGY

$100   WHAT IS THE TELEVISION? $100

$200   WHAT IS A VACUUM CLEANER? $200

$300   WHAT IS A SPACE SHUTTLE? $300

$400   WHAT IS A MICROWAVE OVEN? $400

$500   WHAT IS MS-DOS? $500

JEOPARDY!

"OLD" GLORY

A NURSERY RHYME'S "MERRY OLD SOUL"	$100	WHO IS
A PBS SERIES ONCE HOSTED BY BOB VILA	$200	WHAT IS
A 1952 HEMINGWAY NOVELLA	$300	WHAT IS
GENERAL GEORGE PATTON'S VISCERAL NICKNAME	$400	WHAT IS
ALSO THE TITLE OF A 1595 PLAY, IT'S A TRADITIONAL BELIEF OR STORY THAT'S OFTEN SUPERSTITIOUS	$500	WHAT IS

JEOPARDY!

"OLD" GLORY

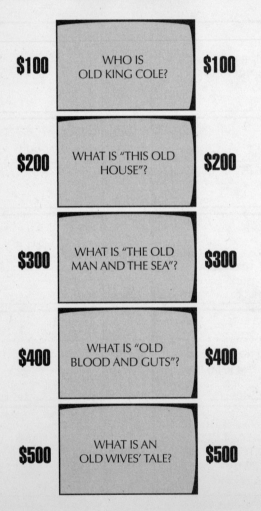

$100 — WHO IS OLD KING COLE? — $100

$200 — WHAT IS "THIS OLD HOUSE"? — $200

$300 — WHAT IS "THE OLD MAN AND THE SEA"? — $300

$400 — WHAT IS "OLD BLOOD AND GUTS"? — $400

$500 — WHAT IS AN OLD WIVES' TALE? — $500

JEOPARDY!

LITTLE-READ BOOKS

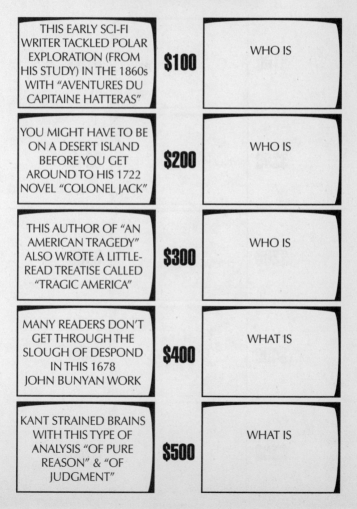

THIS EARLY SCI-FI WRITER TACKLED POLAR EXPLORATION (FROM HIS STUDY) IN THE 1860s WITH "AVENTURES DU CAPITAINE HATTERAS"	$100	WHO IS
YOU MIGHT HAVE TO BE ON A DESERT ISLAND BEFORE YOU GET AROUND TO HIS 1722 NOVEL "COLONEL JACK"	$200	WHO IS
THIS AUTHOR OF "AN AMERICAN TRAGEDY" ALSO WROTE A LITTLE-READ TREATISE CALLED "TRAGIC AMERICA"	$300	WHO IS
MANY READERS DON'T GET THROUGH THE SLOUGH OF DESPOND IN THIS 1678 JOHN BUNYAN WORK	$400	WHAT IS
KANT STRAINED BRAINS WITH THIS TYPE OF ANALYSIS "OF PURE REASON" & "OF JUDGMENT"	$500	WHAT IS

JEOPARDY!

LITTLE-READ BOOKS

$100   WHO IS JULES VERNE? $100

$200   WHO IS DANIEL DEFOE? $200

$300   WHO IS THEODORE DREISER? $300

$400   WHAT IS "THE PILGRIM'S PROGRESS"? $400

$500   WHAT IS A CRITIQUE? $500

DOUBLE JEOPARDY!

HUMANITARIANS

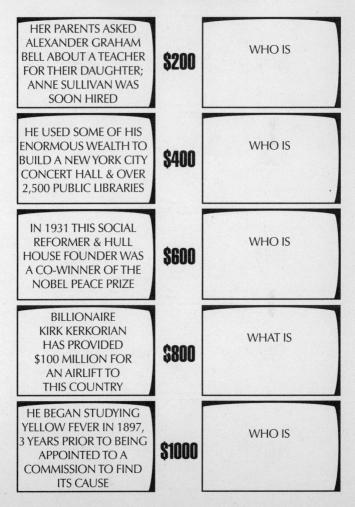

HER PARENTS ASKED ALEXANDER GRAHAM BELL ABOUT A TEACHER FOR THEIR DAUGHTER; ANNE SULLIVAN WAS SOON HIRED	$200	WHO IS
HE USED SOME OF HIS ENORMOUS WEALTH TO BUILD A NEW YORK CITY CONCERT HALL & OVER 2,500 PUBLIC LIBRARIES	$400	WHO IS
IN 1931 THIS SOCIAL REFORMER & HULL HOUSE FOUNDER WAS A CO-WINNER OF THE NOBEL PEACE PRIZE	$600	WHO IS
BILLIONAIRE KIRK KERKORIAN HAS PROVIDED $100 MILLION FOR AN AIRLIFT TO THIS COUNTRY	$800	WHAT IS
HE BEGAN STUDYING YELLOW FEVER IN 1897, 3 YEARS PRIOR TO BEING APPOINTED TO A COMMISSION TO FIND ITS CAUSE	$1000	WHO IS

DOUBLE JEOPARDY!

HUMANITARIANS

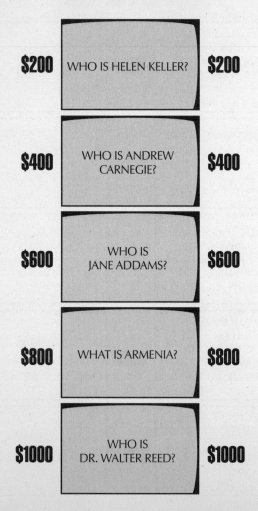

$200   WHO IS HELEN KELLER? $200

$400   WHO IS ANDREW CARNEGIE? $400

$600   WHO IS JANE ADDAMS? $600

$800   WHAT IS ARMENIA? $800

$1000   WHO IS DR. WALTER REED? $1000

DOUBLE JEOPARDY!

TOUGH SHAKESPEARE

ON AN EPISODE OF THE TV SHOW "MOON-LIGHTING", CYBILL SHEPHERD WAS KATE IN AN ADAPTATION OF THIS PLAY	**$200**	WHAT IS
IN THIS COMEDY'S SUBPLOT, SIR TOBY BELCH & MARIA PLAY A TRICK ON MALVOLIO, OLIVIA'S STEWARD	**$400**	WHAT IS
PURSUED BY DEMETRIUS & HELENA, HERMIA & LYSANDER ELOPE TO A WOOD NEAR ATHENS IN THIS COMEDY	**$600**	WHAT IS
COMPLETES SONNET 130's FIRST LINE, "MY MISTRESS' EYES ARE . . ."	**$800**	WHAT IS
IN "KING LEAR" THE EARL OF GLOUCESTER BOASTS OF THIS BASTARD SON: "THERE WAS GOOD SPORT AT HIS MAKING"	**$1000**	WHO IS

DOUBLE JEOPARDY!

TOUGH SHAKESPEARE

$200	WHAT IS "THE TAMING OF THE SHREW"?	$200
$400	WHAT IS "TWELFTH NIGHT (OR, WHAT YOU WILL)"?	$400
$600	WHAT IS "A MID-SUMMER NIGHT'S DREAM"?	$600
$800	WHAT IS "NOTHING LIKE THE SUN"?	$800
$1000	WHO IS EDMUND?	$1000

DOUBLE JEOPARDY!

PLAY BALL!

Clue	Value	Response
THIS EVENT, WHICH HAPPENED MINUTES BEFORE THE START OF GAME 3 IN 1989, POST-PONED THE WORLD SERIES FOR 10 DAYS	$200	WHAT IS
IN 1941 THIS RED SOX OUTFIELDER HIT A SPECTACULAR .406	$400	WHO IS
HALL OF FAMER ROBERTO CLEMENTE SPENT HIS ENTIRE 18-YEAR MAJOR LEAGUE CAREER WITH THIS TEAM	$600	WHAT ARE
NICKNAME OF ALL-STAR THIRD BASEMAN LARRY JONES	$800	WHAT IS
THIS CINCINNATI REDS PLAYER APPEARED IN 3,562 GAMES, THE MOST BY ANY PLAYER IN MAJOR LEAGUE HISTORY	$1000	WHO IS

DOUBLE JEOPARDY!

PLAY BALL!

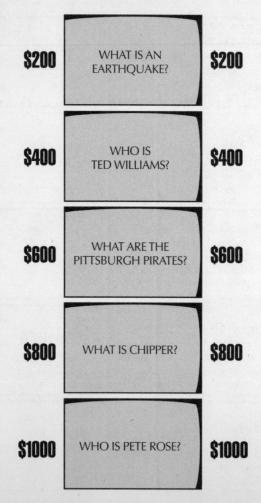

$200 WHAT IS AN EARTHQUAKE? **$200**

$400 WHO IS TED WILLIAMS? **$400**

$600 WHAT ARE THE PITTSBURGH PIRATES? **$600**

$800 WHAT IS CHIPPER? **$800**

$1000 WHO IS PETE ROSE? **$1000**

DOUBLE JEOPARDY!

7-LETTER WORDS

THE ONE THROWN BY MEN IN TRACK & FIELD IS METAL-TIPPED & OVER 8 FEET IN LENGTH	**$200**	WHAT IS
ALTHOUGH FROM FRENCH FOR "MORN-ING", IT NOW REFERS TO A PERFORMANCE IN THE AFTERNOON	**$400**	WHAT IS
THIS FRONT SIDE OF A COIN FEATURES THE PORTRAIT; JEFFERSON ON A NICKEL, FOR EXAMPLE	**$600**	WHAT IS
FROM THE GREEK FOR "STAFF", IT'S A ROD HELD BY A SOVEREIGN AS AN EMBLEM OF POWER OR AUTHORITY	**$800**	WHAT IS
IT'S A MEMBER OF AN ETHNIC GROUP NATIVE TO THE PHILIPPINES, OR THE LANGUAGE ON WHICH PILIPINO IS BASED	**$1000**	WHAT IS

DOUBLE JEOPARDY!

7-LETTER WORDS

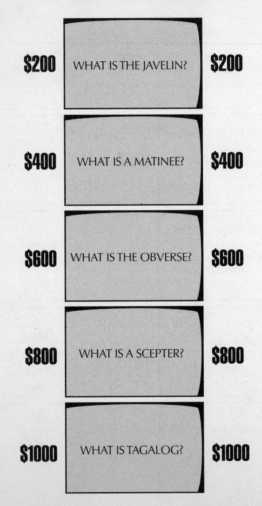

$200   WHAT IS THE JAVELIN?   **$200**

$400   WHAT IS A MATINEE?   **$400**

$600   WHAT IS THE OBVERSE?   **$600**

$800   WHAT IS A SCEPTER?   **$800**

$1000   WHAT IS TAGALOG?   **$1000**

DOUBLE JEOPARDY!

STATE FLOWERS

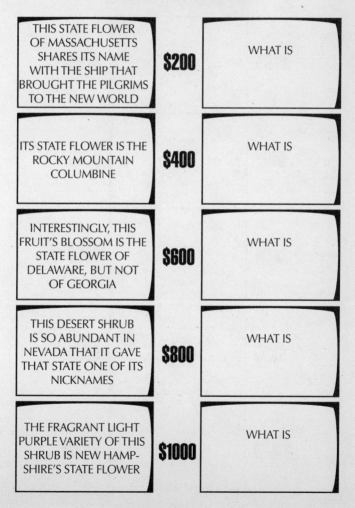

THIS STATE FLOWER OF MASSACHUSETTS SHARES ITS NAME WITH THE SHIP THAT BROUGHT THE PILGRIMS TO THE NEW WORLD	**$200**	WHAT IS
ITS STATE FLOWER IS THE ROCKY MOUNTAIN COLUMBINE	**$400**	WHAT IS
INTERESTINGLY, THIS FRUIT'S BLOSSOM IS THE STATE FLOWER OF DELAWARE, BUT NOT OF GEORGIA	**$600**	WHAT IS
THIS DESERT SHRUB IS SO ABUNDANT IN NEVADA THAT IT GAVE THAT STATE ONE OF ITS NICKNAMES	**$800**	WHAT IS
THE FRAGRANT LIGHT PURPLE VARIETY OF THIS SHRUB IS NEW HAMP-SHIRE'S STATE FLOWER	**$1000**	WHAT IS

DOUBLE JEOPARDY!

STATE FLOWERS

$200   WHAT IS THE MAYFLOWER? $200

$400   WHAT IS COLORADO? $400

$600   WHAT IS THE PEACH? $600

$800   WHAT IS THE SAGEBRUSH? $800

$1000   WHAT IS THE LILAC? $1000

DOUBLE JEOPARDY!

GRANTS

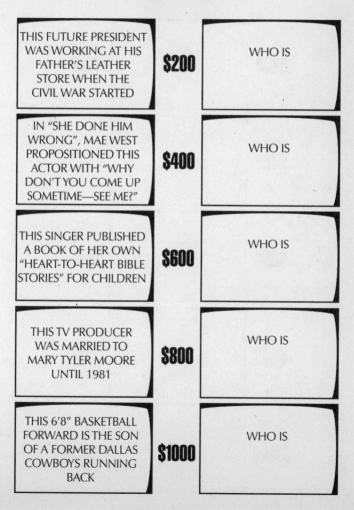

THIS FUTURE PRESIDENT WAS WORKING AT HIS FATHER'S LEATHER STORE WHEN THE CIVIL WAR STARTED	$200	WHO IS
IN "SHE DONE HIM WRONG", MAE WEST PROPOSITIONED THIS ACTOR WITH "WHY DON'T YOU COME UP SOMETIME—SEE ME?"	$400	WHO IS
THIS SINGER PUBLISHED A BOOK OF HER OWN "HEART-TO-HEART BIBLE STORIES" FOR CHILDREN	$600	WHO IS
THIS TV PRODUCER WAS MARRIED TO MARY TYLER MOORE UNTIL 1981	$800	WHO IS
THIS 6'8" BASKETBALL FORWARD IS THE SON OF A FORMER DALLAS COWBOYS RUNNING BACK	$1000	WHO IS

DOUBLE JEOPARDY!

GRANTS

$200   WHO IS ULYSSES S. GRANT? $200

$400   WHO IS CARY GRANT? $400

$600   WHO IS AMY GRANT? $600

$800   WHO IS GRANT TINKER? $800

$1000   WHO IS GRANT HILL? $1000

FINAL JEOPARDY!

ENTERTAINERS

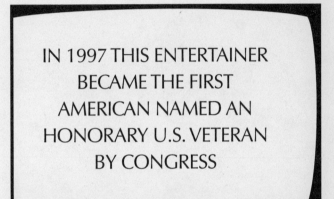

IN 1997 THIS ENTERTAINER
BECAME THE FIRST
AMERICAN NAMED AN
HONORARY U.S. VETERAN
BY CONGRESS

WHO IS

FINAL JEOPARDY!

ENTERTAINERS

WHO IS BOB HOPE?

JEOPARDY!

PARTY TIME!

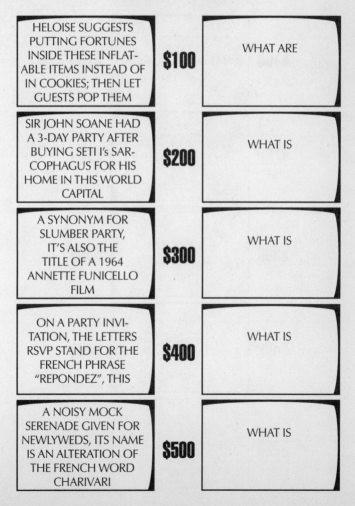

HELOISE SUGGESTS PUTTING FORTUNES INSIDE THESE INFLATABLE ITEMS INSTEAD OF IN COOKIES; THEN LET GUESTS POP THEM	**$100**	WHAT ARE
SIR JOHN SOANE HAD A 3-DAY PARTY AFTER BUYING SETI I's SARCOPHAGUS FOR HIS HOME IN THIS WORLD CAPITAL	**$200**	WHAT IS
A SYNONYM FOR SLUMBER PARTY, IT'S ALSO THE TITLE OF A 1964 ANNETTE FUNICELLO FILM	**$300**	WHAT IS
ON A PARTY INVITATION, THE LETTERS RSVP STAND FOR THE FRENCH PHRASE "REPONDEZ", THIS	**$400**	WHAT IS
A NOISY MOCK SERENADE GIVEN FOR NEWLYWEDS, ITS NAME IS AN ALTERATION OF THE FRENCH WORD CHARIVARI	**$500**	WHAT IS

JEOPARDY!™

PARTY TIME!

$100   WHAT ARE BALLOONS? $100

$200   WHAT IS LONDON? $200

$300   WHAT IS "PAJAMA PARTY"? $300

$400   WHAT IS S'IL VOUS PLAIT? $400

$500   WHAT IS A SHIVAREE? $500

JEOPARDY!

AMERICAN LITERATURE

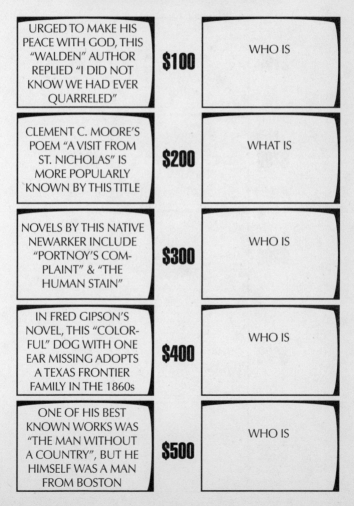

Clue	Value	Response
URGED TO MAKE HIS PEACE WITH GOD, THIS "WALDEN" AUTHOR REPLIED "I DID NOT KNOW WE HAD EVER QUARRELED"	$100	WHO IS
CLEMENT C. MOORE'S POEM "A VISIT FROM ST. NICHOLAS" IS MORE POPULARLY KNOWN BY THIS TITLE	$200	WHAT IS
NOVELS BY THIS NATIVE NEWARKER INCLUDE "PORTNOY'S COMPLAINT" & "THE HUMAN STAIN"	$300	WHO IS
IN FRED GIPSON'S NOVEL, THIS "COLORFUL" DOG WITH ONE EAR MISSING ADOPTS A TEXAS FRONTIER FAMILY IN THE 1860s	$400	WHO IS
ONE OF HIS BEST KNOWN WORKS WAS "THE MAN WITHOUT A COUNTRY", BUT HE HIMSELF WAS A MAN FROM BOSTON	$500	WHO IS

JEOPARDY!

AMERICAN LITERATURE

$100 WHO IS HENRY DAVID THOREAU? **$100**

$200 WHAT IS "('TWAS) THE NIGHT BEFORE CHRISTMAS"? **$200**

$300 WHO IS PHILIP ROTH? **$300**

$400 WHO IS OLD YELLER? **$400**

$500 WHO IS EDWARD EVERETT HALE? **$500**

JEOPARDY!

"SEA" YA

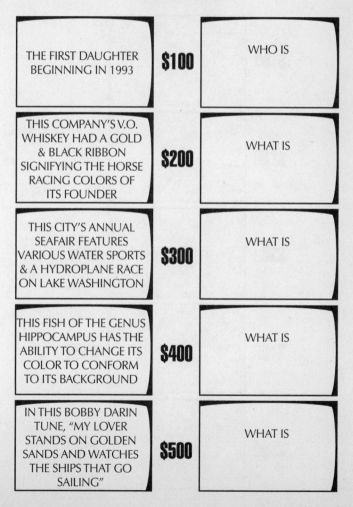

THE FIRST DAUGHTER BEGINNING IN 1993	$100	WHO IS
THIS COMPANY'S V.O. WHISKEY HAD A GOLD & BLACK RIBBON SIGNIFYING THE HORSE RACING COLORS OF ITS FOUNDER	$200	WHAT IS
THIS CITY'S ANNUAL SEAFAIR FEATURES VARIOUS WATER SPORTS & A HYDROPLANE RACE ON LAKE WASHINGTON	$300	WHAT IS
THIS FISH OF THE GENUS HIPPOCAMPUS HAS THE ABILITY TO CHANGE ITS COLOR TO CONFORM TO ITS BACKGROUND	$400	WHAT IS
IN THIS BOBBY DARIN TUNE, "MY LOVER STANDS ON GOLDEN SANDS AND WATCHES THE SHIPS THAT GO SAILING"	$500	WHAT IS

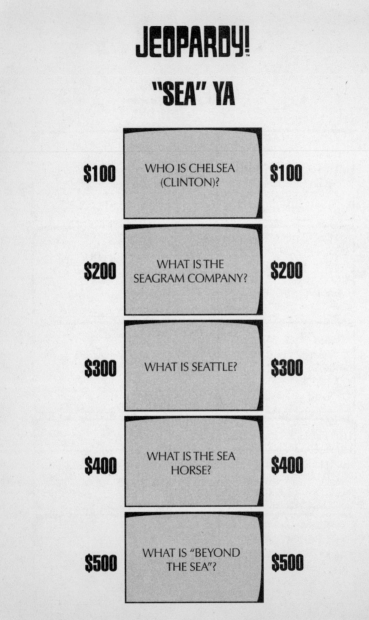

JEOPARDY!

"SEA" YA

$100	WHO IS CHELSEA (CLINTON)?	$100
$200	WHAT IS THE SEAGRAM COMPANY?	$200
$300	WHAT IS SEATTLE?	$300
$400	WHAT IS THE SEA HORSE?	$400
$500	WHAT IS "BEYOND THE SEA"?	$500

JEOPARDY!

ANATOMY

Clue	Value	Response
THE INNER PART OF THIS HAS THE BASILAR MEMBRANE; THE OUTER PART HAS THE LOBE	**$100**	WHAT IS
FROM THE GREEK FOR "BREASTBONE", IT'S, WELL . . . THE BREASTBONE	**$200**	WHAT IS
ALSO CALLED THE PATELLA, IT'S HELD IN PLACE BY A LIGAMENT THAT'S AN EXTENSION OF THE TENDON OF THE THIGH MUSCLE	**$300**	WHAT IS
THIS ORGAN SECRETES GLUCAGON AS WELL AS INSULIN	**$400**	WHAT IS
CINDY CRAWFORD'S MOLE, OR ANYBODY'S, IS A COLLECTION OF CELLS WITH A HIGH CONCENTRATION OF THIS PIGMENT	**$500**	WHAT IS

JEOPARDY!

ANATOMY

$100   WHAT IS THE EAR? $100

$200   WHAT IS THE STERNUM? $200

$300   WHAT IS THE KNEECAP? $300

$400   WHAT IS THE PANCREAS? $400

$500   WHAT IS MELANIN? $500

JEOPARDY!

TV NOSTALGIA

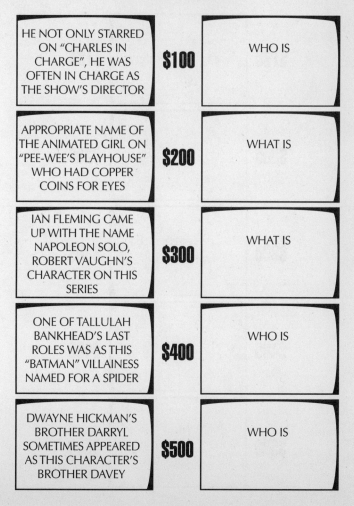

HE NOT ONLY STARRED ON "CHARLES IN CHARGE", HE WAS OFTEN IN CHARGE AS THE SHOW'S DIRECTOR	**$100**	WHO IS
APPROPRIATE NAME OF THE ANIMATED GIRL ON "PEE-WEE'S PLAYHOUSE" WHO HAD COPPER COINS FOR EYES	**$200**	WHAT IS
IAN FLEMING CAME UP WITH THE NAME NAPOLEON SOLO, ROBERT VAUGHN'S CHARACTER ON THIS SERIES	**$300**	WHAT IS
ONE OF TALLULAH BANKHEAD'S LAST ROLES WAS AS THIS "BATMAN" VILLAINESS NAMED FOR A SPIDER	**$400**	WHO IS
DWAYNE HICKMAN'S BROTHER DARRYL SOMETIMES APPEARED AS THIS CHARACTER'S BROTHER DAVEY	**$500**	WHO IS

JEOPARDY!

TV NOSTALGIA

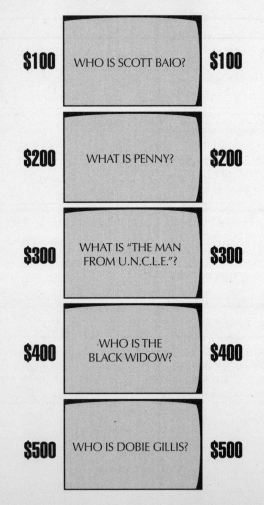

$100 WHO IS SCOTT BAIO? **$100**

$200 WHAT IS PENNY? **$200**

$300 WHAT IS "THE MAN FROM U.N.C.L.E."? **$300**

$400 WHO IS THE BLACK WIDOW? **$400**

$500 WHO IS DOBIE GILLIS? **$500**

JEOPARDY!

WHO THOUGHT OF THAT?

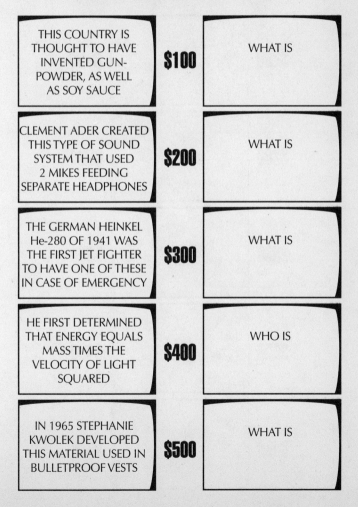

THIS COUNTRY IS THOUGHT TO HAVE INVENTED GUNPOWDER, AS WELL AS SOY SAUCE	$100	WHAT IS
CLEMENT ADER CREATED THIS TYPE OF SOUND SYSTEM THAT USED 2 MIKES FEEDING SEPARATE HEADPHONES	$200	WHAT IS
THE GERMAN HEINKEL He-280 OF 1941 WAS THE FIRST JET FIGHTER TO HAVE ONE OF THESE IN CASE OF EMERGENCY	$300	WHAT IS
HE FIRST DETERMINED THAT ENERGY EQUALS MASS TIMES THE VELOCITY OF LIGHT SQUARED	$400	WHO IS
IN 1965 STEPHANIE KWOLEK DEVELOPED THIS MATERIAL USED IN BULLETPROOF VESTS	$500	WHAT IS

JEOPARDY!

WHO THOUGHT OF THAT?

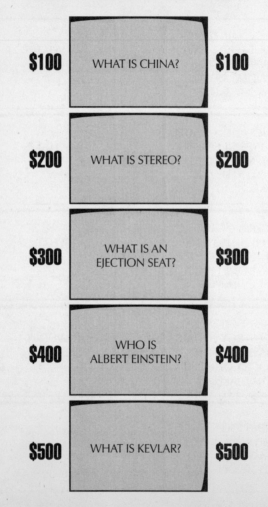

$100   WHAT IS CHINA? $100

$200   WHAT IS STEREO? $200

$300   WHAT IS AN
EJECTION SEAT? $300

$400   WHO IS
ALBERT EINSTEIN? $400

$500   WHAT IS KEVLAR? $500

DOUBLE JEOPARDY!

REDS

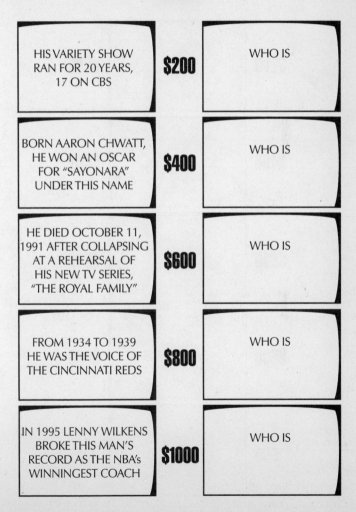

HIS VARIETY SHOW RAN FOR 20 YEARS, 17 ON CBS	$200	WHO IS
BORN AARON CHWATT, HE WON AN OSCAR FOR "SAYONARA" UNDER THIS NAME	$400	WHO IS
HE DIED OCTOBER 11, 1991 AFTER COLLAPSING AT A REHEARSAL OF HIS NEW TV SERIES, "THE ROYAL FAMILY"	$600	WHO IS
FROM 1934 TO 1939 HE WAS THE VOICE OF THE CINCINNATI REDS	$800	WHO IS
IN 1995 LENNY WILKENS BROKE THIS MAN'S RECORD AS THE NBA's WINNINGEST COACH	$1000	WHO IS

DOUBLE JEOPARDY!

REDS

$200   WHO IS RED SKELTON? $200

$400   WHO IS RED BUTTONS? $400

$600   WHO IS REDD FOXX? $600

$800   WHO IS RED BARBER? $800

$1000   WHO IS RED AUERBACH? $1000

DOUBLE JEOPARDY!

HISTORIC NAMES

HIS EPITAPH READS, "FOUNDER OF BOYS TOWN AND LOVER OF CHRIST AND MAN"	**$200**	WHO IS
WHILE ROUNDING THE TIP OF SOUTH AMERICA IN 1520, THIS PORTU-GUESE EXPLORER NAMED CAPE VIRGINES & PATAGONIA	**$400**	WHO IS
IT'S BEEN SAID THAT THE 1831 RUSSIAN CAPTURE OF WARSAW INSPIRED HIM TO WRITE HIS C MINOR ETUDE	**$600**	WHO IS
THIS FAMILY THAT ONCE CONTROLLED NICARA-GUA SAW 2 MEMBERS KILLED—THE FATHER IN 1956, A SON IN 1980	**$800**	WHO ARE
THIS DISCOVERER OF URANUS THOUGHT THE SUN WAS AN INHABITED BODY WITH A LUMI-NOUS ATMOSPHERE	**$1000**	WHO IS

DOUBLE JEOPARDY!

HISTORIC NAMES

$200 · WHO IS FATHER EDWARD FLANAGAN? · $200

$400 · WHO IS FERDINAND MAGELLAN? · $400

$600 · WHO IS FREDERIC CHOPIN? · $600

$800 · WHO ARE THE SOMOZAS? · $800

$1000 · WHO IS WILLIAM HERSCHEL? · $1000

DOUBLE JEOPARDY!

AUSTEN-TATIOUS

JANE AUSTEN SAID ELIZABETH BENNET, THE HEROINE OF THIS NOVEL, WAS "AS DELIGHTFUL A CREATURE AS EVER APPEARED IN PRINT"	$200	WHAT IS
AFTER HER UNSUC-CESSFUL & MEDDLE-SOME MATCHMAKING, THIS TITLE CHARACTER REALIZES SHE LOVES MR. KNIGHTLEY	$400	WHO IS
THIS AUTHOR OF "OR-LANDO" SAID "OF ALL THE GREAT WRITERS" JANE "IS THE MOST DIFFICULT TO CATCH IN THE ACT OF GREATNESS"	$600	WHO IS
WHILE PRINCE REGENT DURING HIS FATHER'S MADNESS, THIS KING HAD A SET OF AUSTEN'S NOVELS IN EACH OF HIS RESIDENCES	$800	WHO IS
THIS TITLE ABBEY IS THE HOME OF CLERGYMAN HENRY TILNEY	$1000	WHAT IS

DOUBLE JEOPARDY!

AUSTEN-TATIOUS

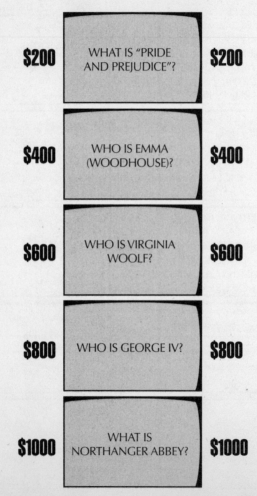

$200 WHAT IS "PRIDE AND PREJUDICE"? **$200**

$400 WHO IS EMMA (WOODHOUSE)? **$400**

$600 WHO IS VIRGINIA WOOLF? **$600**

$800 WHO IS GEORGE IV? **$800**

$1000 WHAT IS NORTHANGER ABBEY? **$1000**

DOUBLE JEOPARDY!

IT'S A GROUP THING

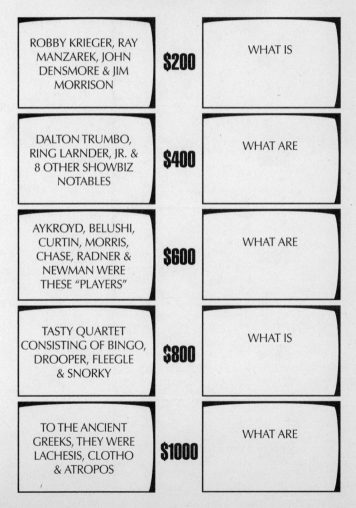

ROBBY KRIEGER, RAY MANZAREK, JOHN DENSMORE & JIM MORRISON	$200	WHAT IS
DALTON TRUMBO, RING LARNDER, JR. & 8 OTHER SHOWBIZ NOTABLES	$400	WHAT ARE
AYKROYD, BELUSHI, CURTIN, MORRIS, CHASE, RADNER & NEWMAN WERE THESE "PLAYERS"	$600	WHAT ARE
TASTY QUARTET CONSISTING OF BINGO, DROOPER, FLEEGLE & SNORKY	$800	WHAT IS
TO THE ANCIENT GREEKS, THEY WERE LACHESIS, CLOTHO & ATROPOS	$1000	WHAT ARE

DOUBLE JEOPARDY!

IT'S A GROUP THING

$200

WHAT IS
THE DOORS?

$200

$400

WHAT ARE THE
HOLLYWOOD TEN?

$400

$600

WHAT ARE THE
NOT READY FOR
PRIME TIME PLAYERS?

$600

$800

WHAT IS THE
BANANA SPLITS?

$800

$1000

WHAT ARE THE FATES?

$1000

DOUBLE JEOPARDY!

PARISIANS

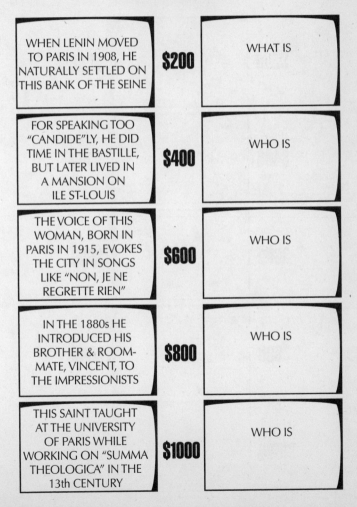

WHEN LENIN MOVED TO PARIS IN 1908, HE NATURALLY SETTLED ON THIS BANK OF THE SEINE	**$200**	WHAT IS
FOR SPEAKING TOO "CANDIDE"LY, HE DID TIME IN THE BASTILLE, BUT LATER LIVED IN A MANSION ON ILE ST-LOUIS	**$400**	WHO IS
THE VOICE OF THIS WOMAN, BORN IN PARIS IN 1915, EVOKES THE CITY IN SONGS LIKE "NON, JE NE REGRETTE RIEN"	**$600**	WHO IS
IN THE 1880s HE INTRODUCED HIS BROTHER & ROOM-MATE, VINCENT, TO THE IMPRESSIONISTS	**$800**	WHO IS
THIS SAINT TAUGHT AT THE UNIVERSITY OF PARIS WHILE WORKING ON "SUMMA THEOLOGICA" IN THE 13th CENTURY	**$1000**	WHO IS

DOUBLE JEOPARDY!

PARISIANS

$200 — WHAT IS THE LEFT BANK? — $200

$400 — WHO IS VOLTAIRE? — $400

$600 — WHO IS EDITH PIAF? — $600

$800 — WHO IS THEO VAN GOGH? — $800

$1000 — WHO IS THOMAS AQUINAS? — $1000

DOUBLE JEOPARDY!

QUESTIONS, QUESTIONS

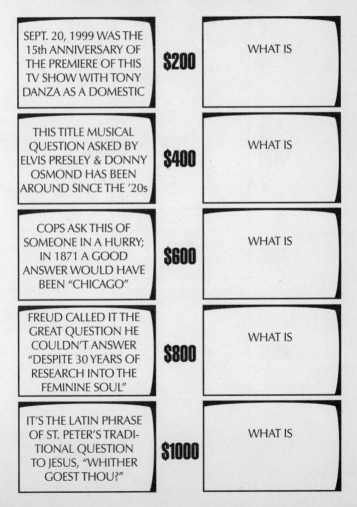

SEPT. 20, 1999 WAS THE 15th ANNIVERSARY OF THE PREMIERE OF THIS TV SHOW WITH TONY DANZA AS A DOMESTIC	**$200**	WHAT IS
THIS TITLE MUSICAL QUESTION ASKED BY ELVIS PRESLEY & DONNY OSMOND HAS BEEN AROUND SINCE THE '20s	**$400**	WHAT IS
COPS ASK THIS OF SOMEONE IN A HURRY; IN 1871 A GOOD ANSWER WOULD HAVE BEEN "CHICAGO"	**$600**	WHAT IS
FREUD CALLED IT THE GREAT QUESTION HE COULDN'T ANSWER "DESPITE 30 YEARS OF RESEARCH INTO THE FEMININE SOUL"	**$800**	WHAT IS
IT'S THE LATIN PHRASE OF ST. PETER'S TRADITIONAL QUESTION TO JESUS, "WHITHER GOEST THOU?"	**$1000**	WHAT IS

DOUBLE JEOPARDY!

QUESTIONS, QUESTIONS

$200   (WHAT IS) "WHO'S THE BOSS?" $200

$400   (WHAT IS) "ARE YOU LONESOME TONIGHT?" $400

$600   (WHAT IS) "WHERE'S THE FIRE?" $600

$800   (WHAT IS) "WHAT DOES A WOMAN (REALLY) WANT?" $800

$1000   (WHAT IS) "QUO VADIS?" $1000

FINAL JEOPARDY!

IN THE KITCHEN

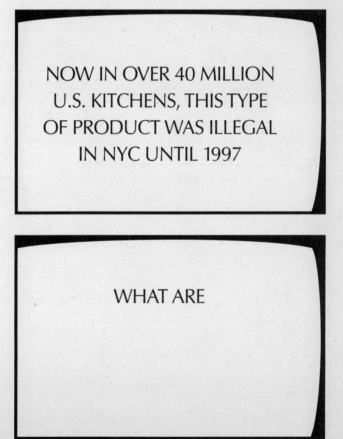

NOW IN OVER 40 MILLION
U.S. KITCHENS, THIS TYPE
OF PRODUCT WAS ILLEGAL
IN NYC UNTIL 1997

WHAT ARE

FINAL JEOPARDY!

IN THE KITCHEN

WHAT ARE
GARBAGE DISPOSALS?

JEOPARDY!

A DRIVING TOUR

DRIVE BY THE COPS WHEN YOU PUT THE PEDAL TO THE METAL ON MOST OF THESE HIGH-SPEED GERMAN HIGHWAYS	**$100**	WHAT ARE
KRASNAYA PLOSHCHAD IS THE LOCAL NAME FOR THIS SQUARE YOU CAN DRIVE BY, BUT NOT ACROSS	**$200**	WHAT IS
HIGH DEGREE FREE-MASONS KNOW IT CAN BE HARD TO DRIVE BY THIS L.A. AUDITORIUM ON JEFFERSON BLVD. ON OSCAR NIGHT	**$300**	WHAT IS
YOU'LL REACH THE PRESIDENT'S OFFICE IN THIS COUNTRY DRIVING TO THE UNION BUILD-INGS ON GOVERNMENT AVE. IN PRETORIA	**$400**	WHAT IS
DRIVE DOWN OBALA VOJVODE STEPE IN THIS CITY & RELIVE THE STREET'S MOST FAMOUS MOMENT OF JUNE 28, 1914	**$500**	WHAT IS

JEOPARDY!

A DRIVING TOUR

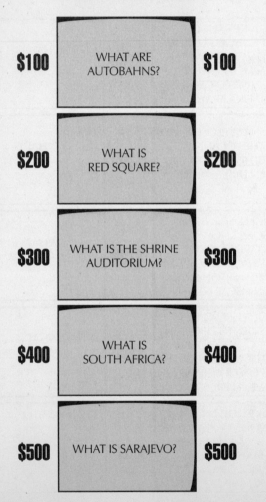

$100 — WHAT ARE AUTOBAHNS? — $100

$200 — WHAT IS RED SQUARE? — $200

$300 — WHAT IS THE SHRINE AUDITORIUM? — $300

$400 — WHAT IS SOUTH AFRICA? — $400

$500 — WHAT IS SARAJEVO? — $500

JEOPARDY!

THE QUOTABLE JOHN ADAMS

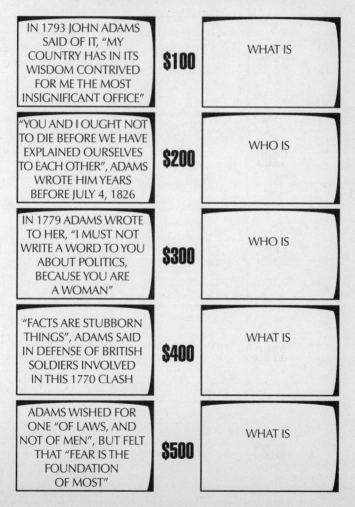

IN 1793 JOHN ADAMS SAID OF IT, "MY COUNTRY HAS IN ITS WISDOM CONTRIVED FOR ME THE MOST INSIGNIFICANT OFFICE"	$100	WHAT IS
"YOU AND I OUGHT NOT TO DIE BEFORE WE HAVE EXPLAINED OURSELVES TO EACH OTHER", ADAMS WROTE HIM YEARS BEFORE JULY 4, 1826	$200	WHO IS
IN 1779 ADAMS WROTE TO HER, "I MUST NOT WRITE A WORD TO YOU ABOUT POLITICS, BECAUSE YOU ARE A WOMAN"	$300	WHO IS
"FACTS ARE STUBBORN THINGS", ADAMS SAID IN DEFENSE OF BRITISH SOLDIERS INVOLVED IN THIS 1770 CLASH	$400	WHAT IS
ADAMS WISHED FOR ONE "OF LAWS, AND NOT OF MEN", BUT FELT THAT "FEAR IS THE FOUNDATION OF MOST"	$500	WHAT IS

JEOPARDY!™

THE QUOTABLE JOHN ADAMS

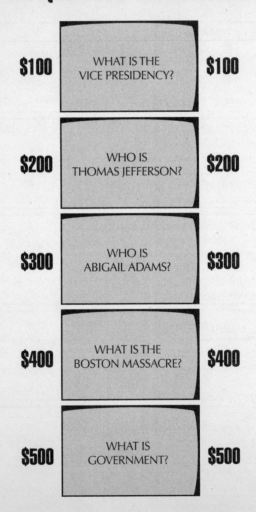

$100 — WHAT IS THE VICE PRESIDENCY? — $100

$200 — WHO IS THOMAS JEFFERSON? — $200

$300 — WHO IS ABIGAIL ADAMS? — $300

$400 — WHAT IS THE BOSTON MASSACRE? — $400

$500 — WHAT IS GOVERNMENT? — $500

JEOPARDY!

ACTORS & ACTRESSES

HER REAL NAME IS DONNA MILLER; ANOTHER ACTRESS HAD THE SAME NAME, SO SHE CHANGED HERS TO THIS	$100	WHAT IS
IN THE 1930s THIS HEARTTHROB WAS SO POPULAR HE WAS KNOWN AS "THE KING OF HOLLYWOOD"	$200	WHO IS
OF JOHN GIELGUD, HENRY IRVING OR LAURENCE OLIVIER, THE FIRST ENGLISH ACTOR TO BE KNIGHTED	$300	WHO IS
THIS "FAIR LADY" OF FILM STARRED ON BROADWAY IN A NON-MUSICAL VERSION OF "GIGI" IN 1951	$400	WHO IS
HE ONCE PLAYED YOUNG TOM HUGHES ON "AS THE WORLD TURNS" BUT HE'S BETTER KNOWN AS JOHN-BOY WALTON	$500	WHO IS

JEOPARDY!

ACTORS & ACTRESSES

$100   WHAT IS DONNA MILLS? $100

$200   WHO IS CLARK GABLE? $200

$300   WHO IS (SIR) HENRY IRVING? $300

$400   WHO IS AUDREY HEPBURN? $400

$500   WHO IS RICHARD THOMAS? $500

JEOPARDY!

EASY AS "PIE"

LITTLE JACK HORNER STUCK HIS THUMB IN THIS & PULLED OUT A PLUM	**$100**	WHAT IS
THIS NO. 1 HIT BY DON McLEAN MOURNED THE DEATH OF BUDDY HOLLY	**$200**	WHAT IS
THIS PHRASE REFERS TO THE DECEPTIVELY ROSY PROSPECT OF FUTURE EVENTS	**$300**	WHAT IS
IT'S A REPRESENTATION OF FACTS PRESENTED AS A CIRCLE DIVIDED INTO SECTORS OF RELATIVE SIZES	**$400**	WHAT IS
CREATED BY PAUL TERRY, THE FAST-TALKING HECKLE & JECKLE ARE 2 OF THESE CROW RELATIVES	**$500**	WHAT ARE

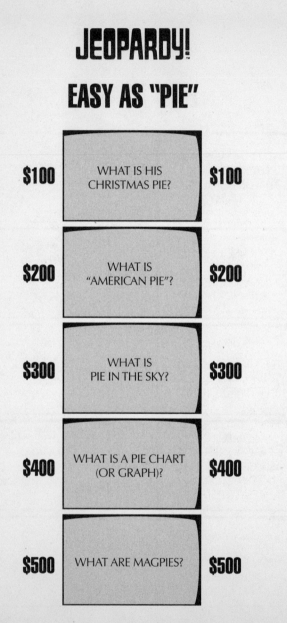

JEOPARDY!

EASY AS "PIE"

$100 — WHAT IS HIS CHRISTMAS PIE? — **$100**

$200 — WHAT IS "AMERICAN PIE"? — **$200**

$300 — WHAT IS PIE IN THE SKY? — **$300**

$400 — WHAT IS A PIE CHART (OR GRAPH)? — **$400**

$500 — WHAT ARE MAGPIES? — **$500**

JEOPARDY!

PUNISHMENT

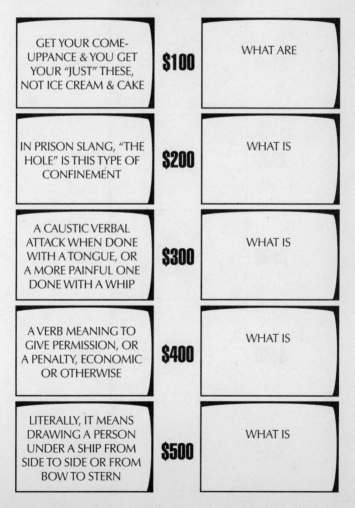

GET YOUR COME-UPPANCE & YOU GET YOUR "JUST" THESE, NOT ICE CREAM & CAKE	**$100**	WHAT ARE
IN PRISON SLANG, "THE HOLE" IS THIS TYPE OF CONFINEMENT	**$200**	WHAT IS
A CAUSTIC VERBAL ATTACK WHEN DONE WITH A TONGUE, OR A MORE PAINFUL ONE DONE WITH A WHIP	**$300**	WHAT IS
A VERB MEANING TO GIVE PERMISSION, OR A PENALTY, ECONOMIC OR OTHERWISE	**$400**	WHAT IS
LITERALLY, IT MEANS DRAWING A PERSON UNDER A SHIP FROM SIDE TO SIDE OR FROM BOW TO STERN	**$500**	WHAT IS

JEOPARDY!

PUNISHMENT

$100	WHAT ARE DESERTS?	**$100**
$200	WHAT IS SOLITARY CONFINEMENT?	**$200**
$300	WHAT IS A LASHING?	**$300**
$400	WHAT IS SANCTION?	**$400**
$500	WHAT IS KEELHAULING?	**$500**

JEOPARDY!

1941

TIME MAGAZINE NAMED THIS ANIMATED BABY ELEPHANT ITS "MAMMAL OF THE YEAR"	**$100**	WHO IS
IN JULY HE WAS MADE LIEUTENANT GENERAL & NAMED COMMANDER IN CHIEF OF ALL U.S. FORCES IN THE FAR EAST	**$200**	WHO IS
TITLE TRAIN IN A 1941 GLENN MILLER HIT	**$300**	WHAT IS
IN 1941 GEORGE HALAS COACHED THIS TEAM TO A 37-9 VICTORY OVER THE NEW YORK GIANTS IN THE NFL TITLE GAME	**$400**	WHAT ARE
IN MAY 1941 HE & HIS COMRADES ORGANIZED THE LEAGUE FOR THE INDEPENDENCE OF VIETNAM	**$500**	WHO IS

JEOPARDY!

1941

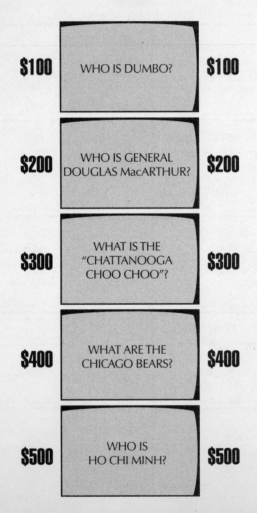

$100 · WHO IS DUMBO? · $100

$200 · WHO IS GENERAL DOUGLAS MacARTHUR? · $200

$300 · WHAT IS THE "CHATTANOOGA CHOO CHOO"? · $300

$400 · WHAT ARE THE CHICAGO BEARS? · $400

$500 · WHO IS HO CHI MINH? · $500

DOUBLE JEOPARDY!

WORD & PHRASE ORIGINS

Clue	Value	Response
THE FRENCH FOR "SCANDAL" GAVE US THE NAME OF THIS HIGH-KICKING DANCE POPULAR IN MUSIC HALLS OF THE 19th CENTURY	$200	WHAT IS
THIS PHRASE FOR TAKING A BREAK FROM A LONG PERIOD OF SITTING GOES BACK TO 19th CENTURY BASEBALL	$400	WHAT IS
AN ILLUSTRATED "GIRL" & A VARIATION ON THE MARTINI ARE NAMED FOR THIS U.S. ARTIST	$600	WHO IS
FROM THE ITALIAN FOR "CHATTER", IT'S A PERSON WHO CLAIMS KNOWLEDGE OR SKILL HE DOESN'T HAVE	$800	WHAT IS
2 GREEK WORDS FOR "LONG LIFE" GIVE US THIS WORD WHICH REFERS TO A DIET OR LIFESTYLE SAID TO PROLONG LIFE	$1000	WHAT IS

DOUBLE JEOPARDY!

WORD & PHRASE ORIGINS

$200   WHAT IS THE CANCAN? $200

$400   WHAT IS THE SEVENTH-INNING STRETCH? $400

$600   WHO IS CHARLES DANA GIBSON? $600

$800   WHAT IS A CHARLATAN? $800

$1000   WHAT IS MACROBIOTIC? $1000

DOUBLE JEOPARDY!

ASTRONOMY

ON FEBRUARY 11, 1999 IT AGAIN BECAME THE FARTHEST PLANET FROM THE SUN & WILL REMAIN SO FOR 248 YEARS	**$200**	WHAT IS
ALNILAM, ALNITAK & MINTAKA ARE THE 3 STARS OF THIS CONSTELLATION'S BELT	**$400**	WHAT IS
AMONG THESE OBJECTS, ENCKE'S HAS AN ORBITAL PERIOD OF 3.3 YEARS; TAGO-SATO-KOSAKA, 420,000 YEARS	**$600**	WHAT ARE
IN 1937 IN WHEATON, ILLINOIS, GROTE REBER BUILT THE FIRST ONE OF THESE TELESCOPES USING A PARABOLIC DISH	**$800**	WHAT IS
THIS ALEXANDRIAN ASTRONOMER DISCUSSES ECLIPSES IN BOOK VI OF HIS 2nd CENTURY WORK "ALMAGEST"	**$1000**	WHO IS

DOUBLE JEOPARDY!

ASTRONOMY

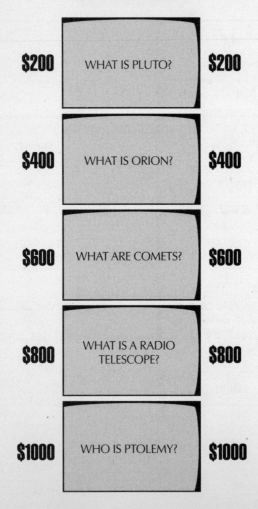

$200   WHAT IS PLUTO? $200

$400   WHAT IS ORION? $400

$600   WHAT ARE COMETS? $600

$800   WHAT IS A RADIO TELESCOPE? $800

$1000   WHO IS PTOLEMY? $1000

DOUBLE JEOPARDY!

COOKING

WHEN A PIE HAS 2 OF THESE, THE TOP ONE MAY BE "WOVEN" IN A LATTICE DESIGN	**$200**	WHAT ARE
DON'T THROW AWAY THIS PART OF A WATERMELON; MANY COOKS PICKLE IT	**$400**	WHAT IS
POPULAR IN ASIA, THIS COOKING UTENSIL THAT USUALLY HAS 2 HANDLES IS PERFECT FOR STIR-FRYING	**$600**	WHAT IS
MIX DRIED, POUNDED MEAT WITH FAT & BERRIES TO MAKE THIS TRADITIONAL FOOD OF NATIVE AMERICANS	**$800**	WHAT IS
THIS TERM FOR A TYPE OF INDIAN COOKING COMES FROM THE NAME OF THE HOT OVEN IT USES	**$1000**	WHAT IS

DOUBLE JEOPARDY!

COOKING

$200	WHAT ARE CRUSTS?	$200
$400	WHAT IS THE RIND?	$400
$600	WHAT IS A WOK?	$600
$800	WHAT IS PEMMICAN?	$800
$1000	WHAT IS TANDOORI?	$1000

DOUBLE JEOPARDY!

ALASKA

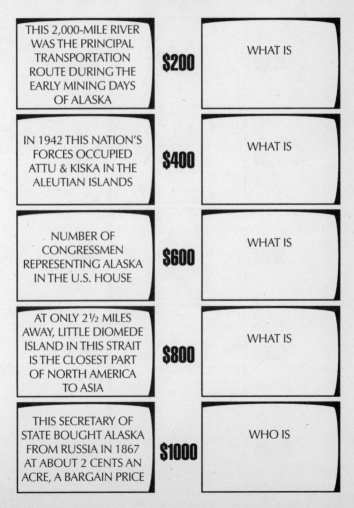

THIS 2,000-MILE RIVER WAS THE PRINCIPAL TRANSPORTATION ROUTE DURING THE EARLY MINING DAYS OF ALASKA	**$200**	WHAT IS
IN 1942 THIS NATION'S FORCES OCCUPIED ATTU & KISKA IN THE ALEUTIAN ISLANDS	**$400**	WHAT IS
NUMBER OF CONGRESSMEN REPRESENTING ALASKA IN THE U.S. HOUSE	**$600**	WHAT IS
AT ONLY 2½ MILES AWAY, LITTLE DIOMEDE ISLAND IN THIS STRAIT IS THE CLOSEST PART OF NORTH AMERICA TO ASIA	**$800**	WHAT IS
THIS SECRETARY OF STATE BOUGHT ALASKA FROM RUSSIA IN 1867 AT ABOUT 2 CENTS AN ACRE, A BARGAIN PRICE	**$1000**	WHO IS

DOUBLE JEOPARDY!

ALASKA

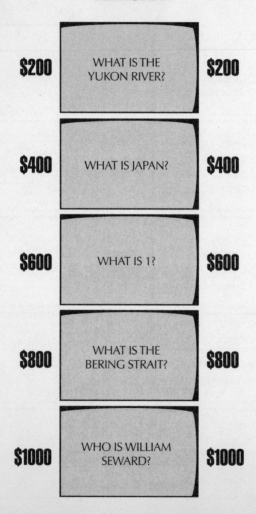

$200 · WHAT IS THE YUKON RIVER? · $200

$400 · WHAT IS JAPAN? · $400

$600 · WHAT IS 1? · $600

$800 · WHAT IS THE BERING STRAIT? · $800

$1000 · WHO IS WILLIAM SEWARD? · $1000

DOUBLE JEOPARDY!

ARCHITECTURE

LUIGI MORETTI DESIGNED BUILDINGS FOR MUSSOLINI & THIS WASHINGTON, D.C. COMPLEX THAT LED TO NIXON'S FALL	**$200**	WHAT IS
THIS STYLE INFLUENCED BY THE ROMANS IS NAMED FOR ENGLAND'S 4 KINGS BETWEEN 1714 & 1830	**$400**	WHAT IS
524 FIRMS COMPETED TO DESIGN A NEW LIBRARY AT THIS CITY TO RECALL THE ANCIENT ONE	**$600**	WHAT IS
HABITAT, BUILT FOR THIS CITY'S EXPO 67, WAS A REVOLUTIONARY PREFABRICATED HOUSING COMPLEX	**$800**	WHAT IS
THIS ARCHITECTURALLY CONTROVERSIAL CENTER NAMED FOR A FRENCH PRESIDENT OPENED IN 1977	**$1000**	WHAT IS

DOUBLE JEOPARDY!

ARCHITECTURE

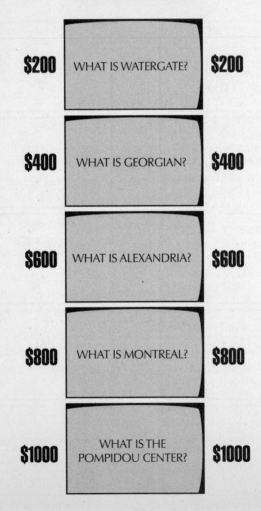

$200   WHAT IS WATERGATE?   **$200**

$400   WHAT IS GEORGIAN?   **$400**

$600   WHAT IS ALEXANDRIA?   **$600**

$800   WHAT IS MONTREAL?   **$800**

$1000   WHAT IS THE POMPIDOU CENTER?   **$1000**

DOUBLE JEOPARDY!

BIG SCREEN BADDIES

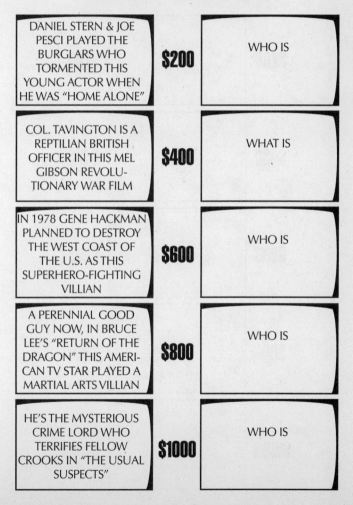

DANIEL STERN & JOE PESCI PLAYED THE BURGLARS WHO TORMENTED THIS YOUNG ACTOR WHEN HE WAS "HOME ALONE"	**$200**	WHO IS
COL. TAVINGTON IS A REPTILIAN BRITISH OFFICER IN THIS MEL GIBSON REVOLUTIONARY WAR FILM	**$400**	WHAT IS
IN 1978 GENE HACKMAN PLANNED TO DESTROY THE WEST COAST OF THE U.S. AS THIS SUPERHERO-FIGHTING VILLIAN	**$600**	WHO IS
A PERENNIAL GOOD GUY NOW, IN BRUCE LEE'S "RETURN OF THE DRAGON" THIS AMERICAN TV STAR PLAYED A MARTIAL ARTS VILLIAN	**$800**	WHO IS
HE'S THE MYSTERIOUS CRIME LORD WHO TERRIFIES FELLOW CROOKS IN "THE USUAL SUSPECTS"	**$1000**	WHO IS

DOUBLE JEOPARDY!

BIG SCREEN BADDIES

$200 WHO IS MACAULAY CULKIN? **$200**

$400 WHAT IS "THE PATRIOT"? **$400**

$600 WHO IS LEX LUTHOR? **$600**

$800 WHO IS CHUCK NORRIS? **$800**

$1000 WHO IS KEYSER SOZE? **$1000**

FINAL JEOPARDY!

CHILDREN'S BOOKS & AUTHORS

HE ALSO CREATED
A 2-LETTER LAND
CALLED IX

WHO IS

FINAL JEOPARDY!

CHILDREN'S BOOKS & AUTHORS

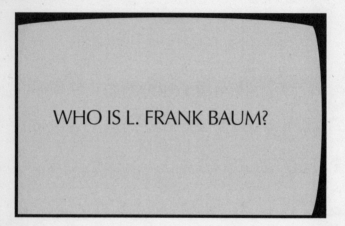

WHO IS L. FRANK BAUM?

JEOPARDY!

JOB BANK

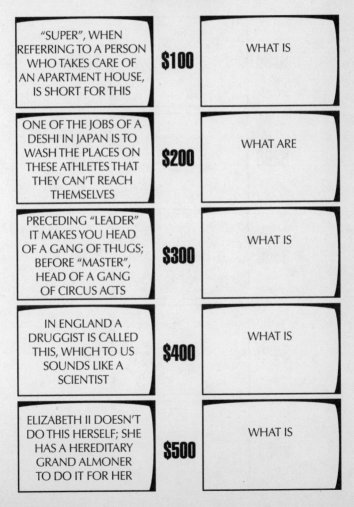

"SUPER", WHEN REFERRING TO A PERSON WHO TAKES CARE OF AN APARTMENT HOUSE, IS SHORT FOR THIS	$100	WHAT IS
ONE OF THE JOBS OF A DESHI IN JAPAN IS TO WASH THE PLACES ON THESE ATHLETES THAT THEY CAN'T REACH THEMSELVES	$200	WHAT ARE
PRECEDING "LEADER" IT MAKES YOU HEAD OF A GANG OF THUGS; BEFORE "MASTER", HEAD OF A GANG OF CIRCUS ACTS	$300	WHAT IS
IN ENGLAND A DRUGGIST IS CALLED THIS, WHICH TO US SOUNDS LIKE A SCIENTIST	$400	WHAT IS
ELIZABETH II DOESN'T DO THIS HERSELF; SHE HAS A HEREDITARY GRAND ALMONER TO DO IT FOR HER	$500	WHAT IS

JEOPARDY!™

JOB BANK

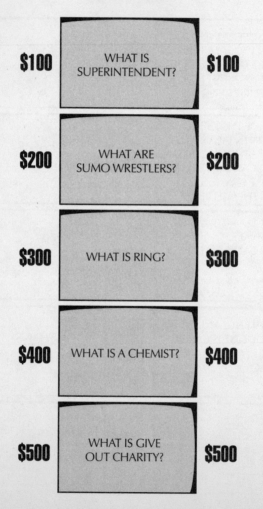

$100 WHAT IS SUPERINTENDENT? **$100**

$200 WHAT ARE SUMO WRESTLERS? **$200**

$300 WHAT IS RING? **$300**

$400 WHAT IS A CHEMIST? **$400**

$500 WHAT IS GIVE OUT CHARITY? **$500**

JEOPARDY!

APRIL

THE CHRISTIAN CELEBRATION OF EASTER & THIS JEWISH FESTIVAL ALSO KNOWN AS PESACH CAN BOTH OCCUR IN APRIL	**$100**	WHAT IS
HE ABDICATED FOR THE FIRST TIME IN APRIL 1814	**$200**	WHO IS
POCAHONTAS MARRIED THIS MAN ON APRIL 5, 1614	**$300**	WHO IS
EACH YEAR ENGLISH-SPEAKING CANADIANS HONOR THIS SAINT ON APRIL 23	**$400**	WHO IS
IN 46 B.C. THIS MAN ORDERED THE ADDITION OF A 30th DAY TO APRIL	**$500**	WHO IS

JEOPARDY!

APRIL

$100 — WHAT IS PASSOVER? — $100

$200 — WHO IS NAPOLEON? — $200

$300 — WHO IS JOHN ROLFE? — $300

$400 — WHO IS ST. GEORGE? — $400

$500 — WHO IS JULIUS CAESAR? — $500

JEOPARDY!

LONG-RUNNING TV SHOWS

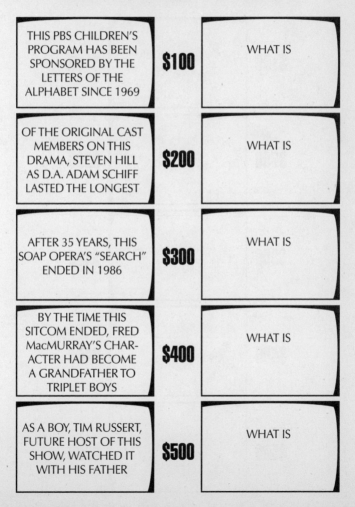

THIS PBS CHILDREN'S PROGRAM HAS BEEN SPONSORED BY THE LETTERS OF THE ALPHABET SINCE 1969	**$100**	WHAT IS
OF THE ORIGINAL CAST MEMBERS ON THIS DRAMA, STEVEN HILL AS D.A. ADAM SCHIFF LASTED THE LONGEST	**$200**	WHAT IS
AFTER 35 YEARS, THIS SOAP OPERA'S "SEARCH" ENDED IN 1986	**$300**	WHAT IS
BY THE TIME THIS SITCOM ENDED, FRED MacMURRAY'S CHARACTER HAD BECOME A GRANDFATHER TO TRIPLET BOYS	**$400**	WHAT IS
AS A BOY, TIM RUSSERT, FUTURE HOST OF THIS SHOW, WATCHED IT WITH HIS FATHER	**$500**	WHAT IS

JEOPARDY!

LONG-RUNNING TV SHOWS

$100 WHAT IS "SESAME STREET"? $100

$200 WHAT IS "LAW & ORDER"? $200

$300 WHAT IS "SEARCH FOR TOMORROW"? $300

$400 WHAT IS "MY THREE SONS"? $400

$500 WHAT IS "MEET THE PRESS"? $500

JEOPARDY!™

FAIRY TALE FEMMES

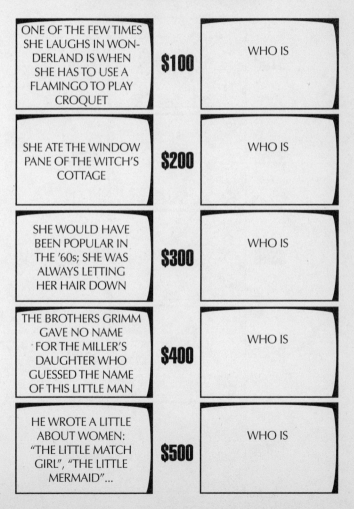

ONE OF THE FEW TIMES SHE LAUGHS IN WONDERLAND IS WHEN SHE HAS TO USE A FLAMINGO TO PLAY CROQUET	$100	WHO IS
SHE ATE THE WINDOW PANE OF THE WITCH'S COTTAGE	$200	WHO IS
SHE WOULD HAVE BEEN POPULAR IN THE '60s; SHE WAS ALWAYS LETTING HER HAIR DOWN	$300	WHO IS
THE BROTHERS GRIMM GAVE NO NAME FOR THE MILLER'S DAUGHTER WHO GUESSED THE NAME OF THIS LITTLE MAN	$400	WHO IS
HE WROTE A LITTLE ABOUT WOMEN: "THE LITTLE MATCH GIRL", "THE LITTLE MERMAID"...	$500	WHO IS

JEOPARDY!

FAIRY TALE FEMMES

$100	WHO IS ALICE?	**$100**
$200	WHO IS GRETEL?	**$200**
$300	WHO IS RAPUNZEL?	**$300**
$400	WHO IS RUMPELSTILTSKIN?	**$400**
$500	WHO IS HANS CHRISTIAN ANDERSEN?	**$500**

JEOPARDY!™

"HORSE" SENSE

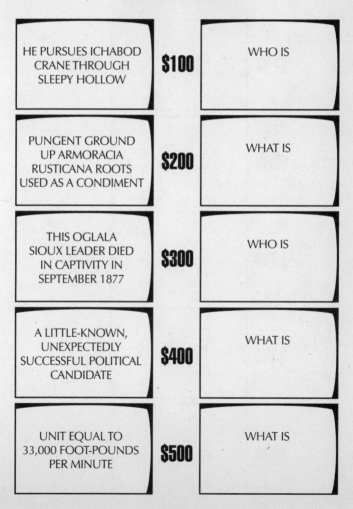

Clue	Value	Answer
HE PURSUES ICHABOD CRANE THROUGH SLEEPY HOLLOW	$100	WHO IS
PUNGENT GROUND UP ARMORACIA RUSTICANA ROOTS USED AS A CONDIMENT	$200	WHAT IS
THIS OGLALA SIOUX LEADER DIED IN CAPTIVITY IN SEPTEMBER 1877	$300	WHO IS
A LITTLE-KNOWN, UNEXPECTEDLY SUCCESSFUL POLITICAL CANDIDATE	$400	WHAT IS
UNIT EQUAL TO 33,000 FOOT-POUNDS PER MINUTE	$500	WHAT IS

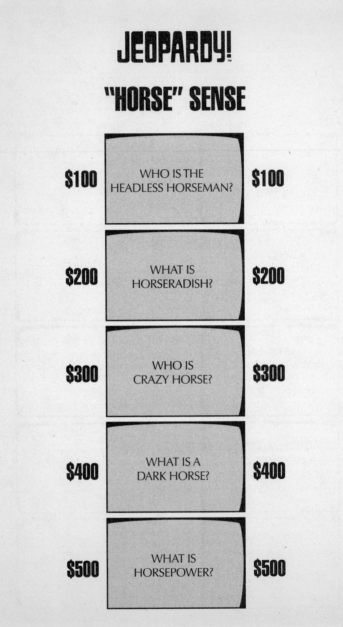

JEOPARDY!

AROUND THE WORLD

BOOMTOWN 1910 IS A RECREATED FRONTIER STREET AT A MUSEUM IN SASKATOON IN THIS CANADIAN PROVINCE	**$100**	WHAT IS
THE EFIK PEOPLE OF THIS CONTINENT ARE CLOSELY RELATED TO THE IBIBIO	**$200**	WHAT IS
COSTA RICA'S NAME TRANSLATES TO THIS IN ENGLISH	**$300**	WHAT IS
THIS SCANDINAVIAN COUNTRY IS QUITE FLAT; ITS HIGHEST POINT, YDING SKOVHOJ, IS JUST 568 HIGH	**$400**	WHAT IS
IF YOU'RE A NATIVE MALDIVIAN, YOU HAIL FROM AN ISLAND COUNTRY IN THIS OCEAN	**$500**	WHAT IS

JEOPARDY!™

AROUND THE WORLD

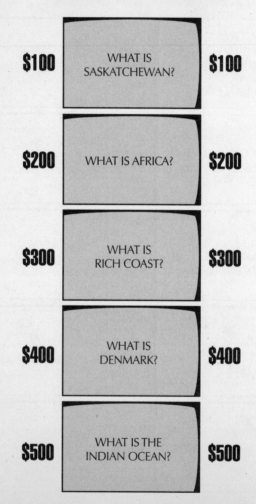

$100   WHAT IS SASKATCHEWAN? $100

$200   WHAT IS AFRICA? $200

$300   WHAT IS RICH COAST? $300

$400   WHAT IS DENMARK? $400

$500   WHAT IS THE INDIAN OCEAN? $500

DOUBLE JEOPARDY!

IT'S ABOUT TIME

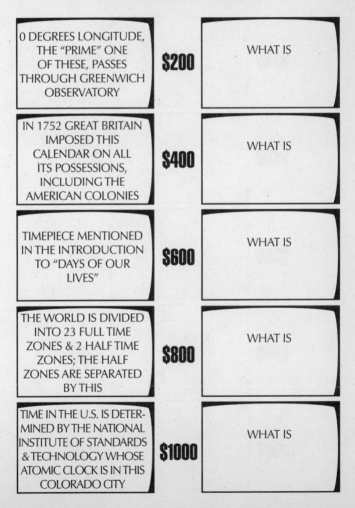

0 DEGREES LONGITUDE, THE "PRIME" ONE OF THESE, PASSES THROUGH GREENWICH OBSERVATORY	$200	WHAT IS
IN 1752 GREAT BRITAIN IMPOSED THIS CALENDAR ON ALL ITS POSSESSIONS, INCLUDING THE AMERICAN COLONIES	$400	WHAT IS
TIMEPIECE MENTIONED IN THE INTRODUCTION TO "DAYS OF OUR LIVES"	$600	WHAT IS
THE WORLD IS DIVIDED INTO 23 FULL TIME ZONES & 2 HALF TIME ZONES; THE HALF ZONES ARE SEPARATED BY THIS	$800	WHAT IS
TIME IN THE U.S. IS DETERMINED BY THE NATIONAL INSTITUTE OF STANDARDS & TECHNOLOGY WHOSE ATOMIC CLOCK IS IN THIS COLORADO CITY	$1000	WHAT IS

DOUBLE JEOPARDY!

IT'S ABOUT TIME

$200 WHAT IS THE PRIME MERIDIAN? **$200**

$400 WHAT IS THE GREGORIAN CALENDAR? **$400**

$600 WHAT IS AN HOURGLASS? **$600**

$800 WHAT IS THE INTERNATIONAL DATE LINE? **$800**

$1000 WHAT IS BOULDER? **$1000**

DOUBLE JEOPARDY!

ASIAN CITIES

Clue	Value	Response
IN A 1940 FILM SABU WAS "THE THIEF OF" THIS CITY	$200	WHAT IS
YOU COULD CALL BENAZIR BHUTTO, BORN IN THIS COUNTRY'S LARGEST CITY, THE KARACHI KID	$400	WHAT IS
IT HOSTED THE 1972 WINTER OLYMPICS & LENDS ITS NAME TO ONE OF JAPAN'S OLDEST BRANDS OF BEER	$600	WHAT IS
IN THIS CITY YOU CAN VISIT AN UPLIFTING MUSEUM OF KHMER ART, OR TUOL SLENG, A MUSEUM OF TORTURE & MURDER	$800	WHAT IS
UH, JUST ONE MORE THING ... IT'S SRI LANKA'S MOST IMPORTANT PORT	$1000	WHAT IS

DOUBLE JEOPARDY!

ASIAN CITIES

$200 WHAT IS BAGHDAD? $200

$400 WHAT IS PAKISTAN? $400

$600 WHAT IS SAPPORO? $600

$800 WHAT IS PHNOM PENH? $800

$1000 WHAT IS COLOMBO? $1000

DOUBLE JEOPARDY!

RHYMES WITH RAIN

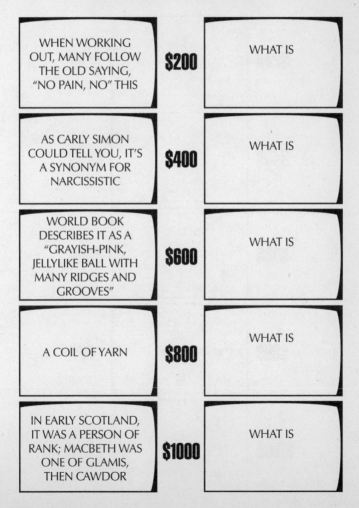

WHEN WORKING OUT, MANY FOLLOW THE OLD SAYING, "NO PAIN, NO" THIS	$200	WHAT IS
AS CARLY SIMON COULD TELL YOU, IT'S A SYNONYM FOR NARCISSISTIC	$400	WHAT IS
WORLD BOOK DESCRIBES IT AS A "GRAYISH-PINK, JELLYLIKE BALL WITH MANY RIDGES AND GROOVES"	$600	WHAT IS
A COIL OF YARN	$800	WHAT IS
IN EARLY SCOTLAND, IT WAS A PERSON OF RANK; MACBETH WAS ONE OF GLAMIS, THEN CAWDOR	$1000	WHAT IS

DOUBLE JEOPARDY!

RHYMES WITH RAIN

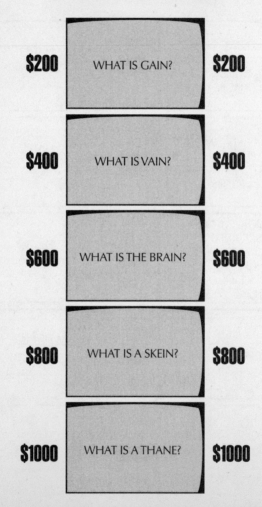

$200	WHAT IS GAIN?	$200
$400	WHAT IS VAIN?	$400
$600	WHAT IS THE BRAIN?	$600
$800	WHAT IS A SKEIN?	$800
$1000	WHAT IS A THANE?	$1000

DOUBLE JEOPARDY!

THE SOCIAL SCIENCES

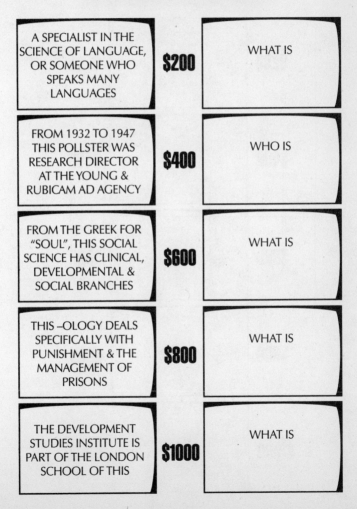

A SPECIALIST IN THE SCIENCE OF LANGUAGE, OR SOMEONE WHO SPEAKS MANY LANGUAGES	**$200**	WHAT IS
FROM 1932 TO 1947 THIS POLLSTER WAS RESEARCH DIRECTOR AT THE YOUNG & RUBICAM AD AGENCY	**$400**	WHO IS
FROM THE GREEK FOR "SOUL", THIS SOCIAL SCIENCE HAS CLINICAL, DEVELOPMENTAL & SOCIAL BRANCHES	**$600**	WHAT IS
THIS –OLOGY DEALS SPECIFICALLY WITH PUNISHMENT & THE MANAGEMENT OF PRISONS	**$800**	WHAT IS
THE DEVELOPMENT STUDIES INSTITUTE IS PART OF THE LONDON SCHOOL OF THIS	**$1000**	WHAT IS

DOUBLE JEOPARDY!

THE SOCIAL SCIENCES

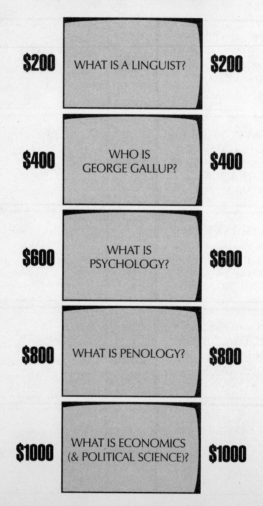

$200   WHAT IS A LINGUIST? $200

$400   WHO IS GEORGE GALLUP? $400

$600   WHAT IS PSYCHOLOGY? $600

$800   WHAT IS PENOLOGY? $800

$1000   WHAT IS ECONOMICS (& POLITICAL SCIENCE)? $1000

DOUBLE JEOPARDY!

ART & ARTISTS

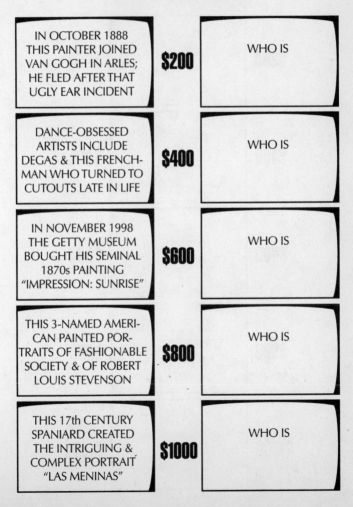

IN OCTOBER 1888 THIS PAINTER JOINED VAN GOGH IN ARLES; HE FLED AFTER THAT UGLY EAR INCIDENT	**$200**	WHO IS
DANCE-OBSESSED ARTISTS INCLUDE DEGAS & THIS FRENCH-MAN WHO TURNED TO CUTOUTS LATE IN LIFE	**$400**	WHO IS
IN NOVEMBER 1998 THE GETTY MUSEUM BOUGHT HIS SEMINAL 1870s PAINTING "IMPRESSION: SUNRISE"	**$600**	WHO IS
THIS 3-NAMED AMERI-CAN PAINTED POR-TRAITS OF FASHIONABLE SOCIETY & OF ROBERT LOUIS STEVENSON	**$800**	WHO IS
THIS 17th CENTURY SPANIARD CREATED THE INTRIGUING & COMPLEX PORTRAIT "LAS MENINAS"	**$1000**	WHO IS

DOUBLE JEOPARDY!

ART & ARTISTS

$200 WHO IS PAUL GAUGUIN? **$200**

$400 WHO IS HENRI MATISSE? **$400**

$600 WHO IS CLAUDE MONET? **$600**

$800 WHO IS JOHN SINGER SARGENT? **$800**

$1000 WHO IS DIEGO VELAZQUEZ? **$1000**

DOUBLE JEOPARDY!

MICHELLE PFEIFFER PFILMS

Clue	Value	Response
TZIPPORAH, THE FUTURE BRIDE OF MOSES, WAS VOICE BY MICHELLE IN THIS 1998 ANIMATED FILM	$200	WHAT IS
ONE OF MICHELLE'S 2 FILMS WITH "DANGEROUS" IN THE TITLE	$400	WHAT IS
MICHELLE LIVENED UP THE LOUNGE ACT OF PIANO-PLAYING BROTHERS BEAU & JEFF BRIDGES IN THIS FILM	$600	WHAT IS
MICHELLE TRIES TO ESCAPE FROM THE MAFIA AFTER THE DEATH OF HER HIT-MAN HUSBAND IN THIS 1988 COMEDY	$800	WHAT IS
BOOK EDITOR JACK NICHOLSON GETS INTO SOME "HAIRY" SITUATIONS WITH MICHELLE IN THIS 1994 THRILLER	$1000	WHAT IS

DOUBLE JEOPARDY!

MICHELLE PFEIFFER PFILMS

$200 · WHAT IS "THE PRINCE OF EGYPT"? · $200

$400 · WHAT IS "DANGEROUS LIAISONS" OR "DANGEROUS MINDS"? · $400

$600 · WHAT IS "THE FABULOUS BAKER BOYS"? · $600

$800 · WHAT IS "MARRIED TO THE MOB"? · $800

$1000 · WHAT IS "WOLF"? · $1000

FINAL JEOPARDY!

AVIATION

ON OCTOBER 14, 1997 HE
RE-CREATED A FEAT HE HAD
PERFORMED EXACTLY FIFTY
YEARS EARLIER

WHO IS

FINAL JEOPARDY!

AVIATION

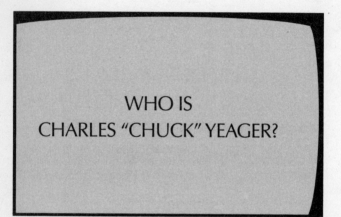

WHO IS
CHARLES "CHUCK" YEAGER?

JEOPARDY!

TV THROUGH THE YEARS

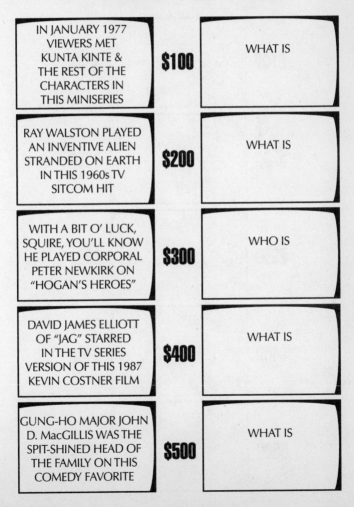

IN JANUARY 1977 VIEWERS MET KUNTA KINTE & THE REST OF THE CHARACTERS IN THIS MINISERIES	**$100**	WHAT IS
RAY WALSTON PLAYED AN INVENTIVE ALIEN STRANDED ON EARTH IN THIS 1960s TV SITCOM HIT	**$200**	WHAT IS
WITH A BIT O' LUCK, SQUIRE, YOU'LL KNOW HE PLAYED CORPORAL PETER NEWKIRK ON "HOGAN'S HEROES"	**$300**	WHO IS
DAVID JAMES ELLIOTT OF "JAG" STARRED IN THE TV SERIES VERSION OF THIS 1987 KEVIN COSTNER FILM	**$400**	WHAT IS
GUNG-HO MAJOR JOHN D. MacGILLIS WAS THE SPIT-SHINED HEAD OF THE FAMILY ON THIS COMEDY FAVORITE	**$500**	WHAT IS

JEOPARDY!

TV THROUGH THE YEARS

$100 — WHAT IS "ROOTS"? — $100

$200 — WHAT IS "MY FAVORITE MARTIAN"? — $200

$300 — WHO IS RICHARD DAWSON? — $300

$400 — WHAT IS "THE UNTOUCHABLES"? — $400

$500 — WHAT IS "MAJOR DAD"? — $500

JEOPARDY!

FAMOUS FEUDS

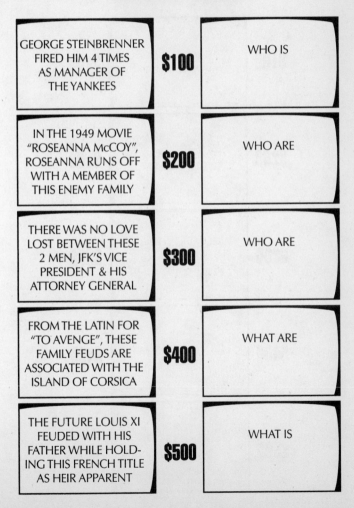

GEORGE STEINBRENNER FIRED HIM 4 TIMES AS MANAGER OF THE YANKEES	**$100**	WHO IS
IN THE 1949 MOVIE "ROSEANNA McCOY", ROSEANNA RUNS OFF WITH A MEMBER OF THIS ENEMY FAMILY	**$200**	WHO ARE
THERE WAS NO LOVE LOST BETWEEN THESE 2 MEN, JFK'S VICE PRESIDENT & HIS ATTORNEY GENERAL	**$300**	WHO ARE
FROM THE LATIN FOR "TO AVENGE", THESE FAMILY FEUDS ARE ASSOCIATED WITH THE ISLAND OF CORSICA	**$400**	WHAT ARE
THE FUTURE LOUIS XI FEUDED WITH HIS FATHER WHILE HOLDING THIS FRENCH TITLE AS HEIR APPARENT	**$500**	WHAT IS

JEOPARDY!™

FAMOUS FEUDS

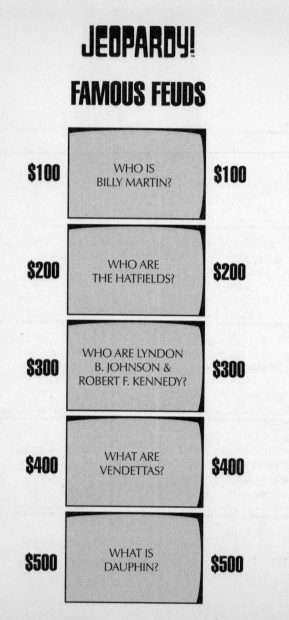

$100   WHO IS BILLY MARTIN? $100

$200   WHO ARE THE HATFIELDS? $200

$300   WHO ARE LYNDON B. JOHNSON & ROBERT F. KENNEDY? $300

$400   WHAT ARE VENDETTAS? $400

$500   WHAT IS DAUPHIN? $500

JEOPARDY!

COMMUNISM

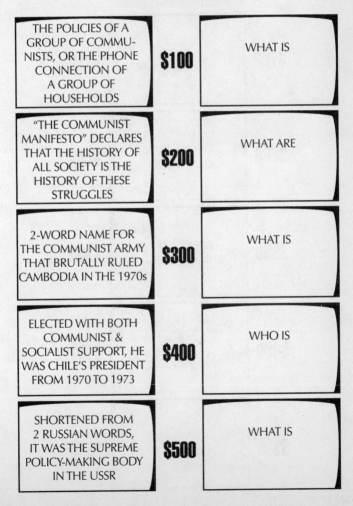

THE POLICIES OF A GROUP OF COMMUNISTS, OR THE PHONE CONNECTION OF A GROUP OF HOUSEHOLDS	$100	WHAT IS
"THE COMMUNIST MANIFESTO" DECLARES THAT THE HISTORY OF ALL SOCIETY IS THE HISTORY OF THESE STRUGGLES	$200	WHAT ARE
2-WORD NAME FOR THE COMMUNIST ARMY THAT BRUTALLY RULED CAMBODIA IN THE 1970s	$300	WHAT IS
ELECTED WITH BOTH COMMUNIST & SOCIALIST SUPPORT, HE WAS CHILE'S PRESIDENT FROM 1970 TO 1973	$400	WHO IS
SHORTENED FROM 2 RUSSIAN WORDS, IT WAS THE SUPREME POLICY-MAKING BODY IN THE USSR	$500	WHAT IS

JEOPARDY!

COMMUNISM

$100 — WHAT IS THE PARTY LINE? — $100

$200 — WHAT ARE CLASS STRUGGLES? — $200

$300 — WHAT IS THE KHMER ROUGE? — $300

$400 — WHO IS SALVADOR ALLENDE? — $400

$500 — WHAT IS THE POLITBURO? — $500

JEOPARDY!

GOOD PROVERBS

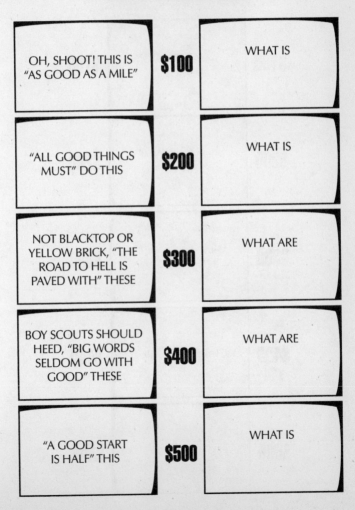

OH, SHOOT! THIS IS "AS GOOD AS A MILE"	**$100**	WHAT IS
"ALL GOOD THINGS MUST" DO THIS	**$200**	WHAT IS
NOT BLACKTOP OR YELLOW BRICK, "THE ROAD TO HELL IS PAVED WITH" THESE	**$300**	WHAT ARE
BOY SCOUTS SHOULD HEED, "BIG WORDS SELDOM GO WITH GOOD" THESE	**$400**	WHAT ARE
"A GOOD START IS HALF" THIS	**$500**	WHAT IS

JEOPARDY!

GOOD PROVERBS

$100 — WHAT IS "A MISS"? — $100

$200 — WHAT IS "COME TO AN END"? — $200

$300 — WHAT ARE "GOOD INTENTIONS"? — $300

$400 — WHAT ARE "DEEDS"? — $400

$500 — WHAT IS "THE RACE"? — $500

JEOPARDY!

FOR WHAT IT'S WORDSWORTH

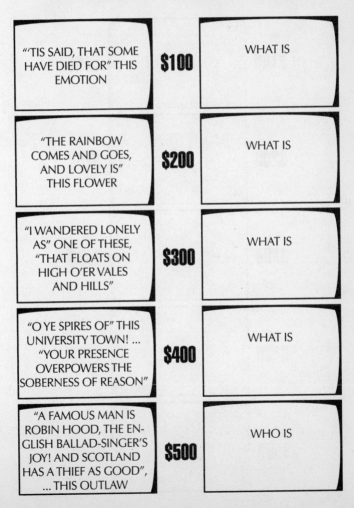

Clue	Value	Response
"'TIS SAID, THAT SOME HAVE DIED FOR" THIS EMOTION	$100	WHAT IS
"THE RAINBOW COMES AND GOES, AND LOVELY IS" THIS FLOWER	$200	WHAT IS
"I WANDERED LONELY AS" ONE OF THESE, "THAT FLOATS ON HIGH O'ER VALES AND HILLS"	$300	WHAT IS
"O YE SPIRES OF" THIS UNIVERSITY TOWN! ... "YOUR PRESENCE OVERPOWERS THE SOBERNESS OF REASON"	$400	WHAT IS
"A FAMOUS MAN IS ROBIN HOOD, THE ENGLISH BALLAD-SINGER'S JOY! AND SCOTLAND HAS A THIEF AS GOOD", ... THIS OUTLAW	$500	WHO IS

JEOPARDY!

FOR WHAT IT'S WORDSWORTH

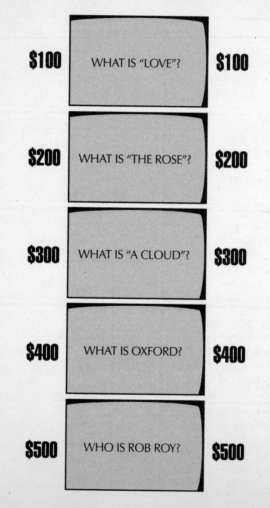

$100   WHAT IS "LOVE"? $100

$200   WHAT IS "THE ROSE"? $200

$300   WHAT IS "A CLOUD"? $300

$400   WHAT IS OXFORD? $400

$500   WHO IS ROB ROY? $500

JEOPARDY!

THE HUDSON RIVER

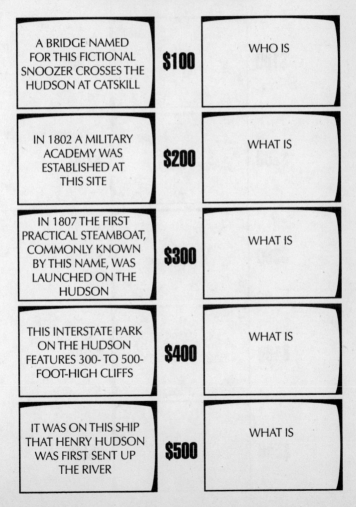

A BRIDGE NAMED FOR THIS FICTIONAL SNOOZER CROSSES THE HUDSON AT CATSKILL	**$100**	WHO IS
IN 1802 A MILITARY ACADEMY WAS ESTABLISHED AT THIS SITE	**$200**	WHAT IS
IN 1807 THE FIRST PRACTICAL STEAMBOAT, COMMONLY KNOWN BY THIS NAME, WAS LAUNCHED ON THE HUDSON	**$300**	WHAT IS
THIS INTERSTATE PARK ON THE HUDSON FEATURES 300- TO 500-FOOT-HIGH CLIFFS	**$400**	WHAT IS
IT WAS ON THIS SHIP THAT HENRY HUDSON WAS FIRST SENT UP THE RIVER	**$500**	WHAT IS

JEOPARDY!

THE HUDSON RIVER

$100	WHO IS RIP VAN WINKLE?	**$100**
$200	WHAT IS WEST POINT?	**$200**
$300	WHAT IS THE CLERMONT?	**$300**
$400	WHAT IS PALISADES INTERSTATE PARK?	**$400**
$500	WHAT IS THE HALF MOON?	**$500**

DOUBLE JEOPARDY!

IMMIGRANTS FROM RUSSIA

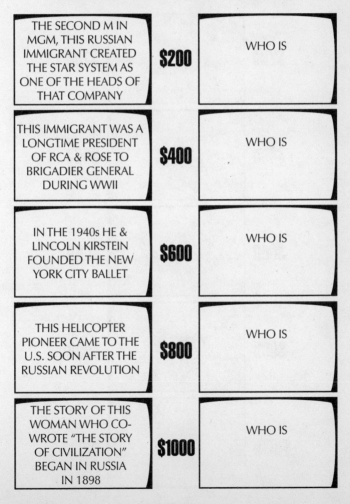

THE SECOND M IN MGM, THIS RUSSIAN IMMIGRANT CREATED THE STAR SYSTEM AS ONE OF THE HEADS OF THAT COMPANY	$200	WHO IS
THIS IMMIGRANT WAS A LONGTIME PRESIDENT OF RCA & ROSE TO BRIGADIER GENERAL DURING WWII	$400	WHO IS
IN THE 1940s HE & LINCOLN KIRSTEIN FOUNDED THE NEW YORK CITY BALLET	$600	WHO IS
THIS HELICOPTER PIONEER CAME TO THE U.S. SOON AFTER THE RUSSIAN REVOLUTION	$800	WHO IS
THE STORY OF THIS WOMAN WHO CO-WROTE "THE STORY OF CIVILIZATION" BEGAN IN RUSSIA IN 1898	$1000	WHO IS

DOUBLE JEOPARDY!

IMMIGRANTS FROM RUSSIA

$200   WHO IS
LOUIS B. MAYER?   **$200**

$400   WHO IS
DAVID SARNOFF?   **$400**

$600   WHO IS
GEORGE BALANCHINE?   **$600**

$800   WHO IS
IGOR SIKORSKY?   **$800**

$1000   WHO IS
ARIEL DURANT?   **$1000**

DOUBLE JEOPARDY!

JUNE SWOON

Clue	Value	Response
ONE OF THE 2 DAYS ON WHICH SUMMER CAN BEGIN IN THE NORTHERN HEMISPHERE	$200	WHAT ARE
THIS WAR BEGAN WITH AN ATTACK ACROSS THE 38th PARALLEL ON JUNE 25, 1950	$400	WHAT IS
AFTER A REVOLT IN ALGERIA, THIS MAN BECAME PREMIER OF FRANCE IN JUNE 1958 WITH ALMOST UNLIMITED AUTHORITY	$600	WHO IS
THE ROMANS NAMED THE MONTH FOR JUNO, PATRON GODDESS OF WOMEN & THIS SOCIAL RITE	$800	WHAT IS
ON JUNE 4 THIS COUNTRY HONORS CARL GUSTAF MANNER-HEIM, A LEADER IN ITS FIGHT FOR INDEPEN-DENCE FROM RUSSIA	$1000	WHAT IS

145

DOUBLE JEOPARDY!

JUNE SWOON

$200	WHAT ARE JUNE 21 OR JUNE 22?	$200
$400	WHAT IS THE KOREAN WAR?	$400
$600	WHO IS CHARLES DE GAULLE?	$600
$800	WHAT IS MARRIAGE?	$800
$1000	WHAT IS FINLAND?	$1000

DOUBLE JEOPARDY!

JACKSON ACTION

THIS GENERAL GAINED HIS FAMOUS NICKNAME AT THE FIRST BATTLE OF BULL RUN	**$200**	WHO IS
IN 1971 THIS BAPTIST MINISTER FOUNDED OPERATION PUSH (PEOPLE UNITED TO SAVE HUMANITY)	**$400**	WHO IS
"WHOA, NELLIE!" IS A CATCHPHRASE OF THIS LEGENDARY SPORTSCASTER	**$600**	WHO IS
THIS BRITISH ACTRESS & LABOUR POLITICIAN SAID, "ACTING IS NOT ABOUT DRESSING UP" BUT "ABOUT STRIPPING BARE"	**$800**	WHO IS
IN OCTOBER 1973 HE BECAME THE FIRST BLACK MAYOR OF ATLANTA, GEORGIA	**$1000**	WHO IS

DOUBLE JEOPARDY!

JACKSON ACTION

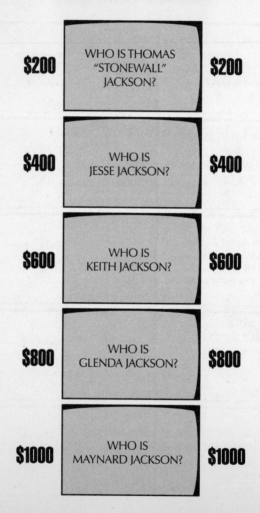

$200 — WHO IS THOMAS "STONEWALL" JACKSON? — $200

$400 — WHO IS JESSE JACKSON? — $400

$600 — WHO IS KEITH JACKSON? — $600

$800 — WHO IS GLENDA JACKSON? — $800

$1000 — WHO IS MAYNARD JACKSON? — $1000

DOUBLE JEOPARDY!

CROSSWORD CLUES "G"

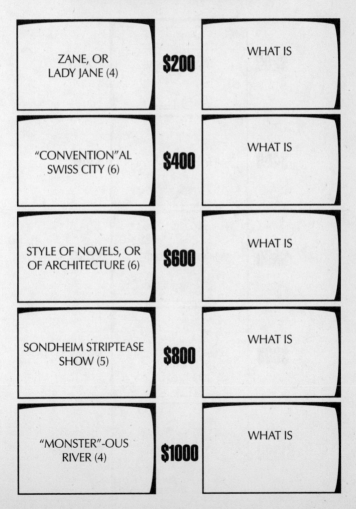

Clue	Value	Response
ZANE, OR LADY JANE (4)	$200	WHAT IS
"CONVENTION"AL SWISS CITY (6)	$400	WHAT IS
STYLE OF NOVELS, OR OF ARCHITECTURE (6)	$600	WHAT IS
SONDHEIM STRIPTEASE SHOW (5)	$800	WHAT IS
"MONSTER"-OUS RIVER (4)	$1000	WHAT IS

DOUBLE JEOPARDY!

CROSSWORD CLUES "G"

$200 — WHAT IS GREY? — **$200**

$400 — WHAT IS GENEVA? — **$400**

$600 — WHAT IS GOTHIC? — **$600**

$800 — WHAT IS "GYPSY"? — **$800**

$1000 — WHAT IS GILA? — **$1000**

DOUBLE JEOPARDY!

PENINSULAS

THE REGION OF APULIA OCCUPIES THE "HEEL" OF THIS PENINSULA	**$200**	WHAT IS
COLOMBIA & VENEZUELA SHARE THE GUAJIRA PENINSULA, WHICH JUTS INTO THIS SEA	**$400**	WHAT IS
THE PENINSULA AT THE NORTHWESTERN EDGE OF THIS CONTINENT HAS BEEN CLAIMED BY ENGLAND, CHILE & ARGENTINA	**$600**	WHAT IS
MENTION THE EAST SIDE OF AUSTRALIA'S CAPE YORK PENINSULA & YOU'RE "REEF"ERRING TO THIS SEA	**$800**	WHAT IS
THE RAMONES SANG ABOUT THIS BEACH IN QUEENS THAT'S ON A PENINSULA OF THE SAME NAME	**$1000**	WHAT IS

DOUBLE JEOPARDY!

PENINSULAS

$200 — WHAT IS THE ITALIAN PENINSULA? — $200

$400 — WHAT IS THE CARIBBEAN? — $400

$600 — WHAT IS ANTARCTICA? — $600

$800 — WHAT IS THE CORAL SEA? — $800

$1000 — WHAT IS ROCKAWAY BEACH? — $1000

DOUBLE JEOPARDY!

MINIVANS

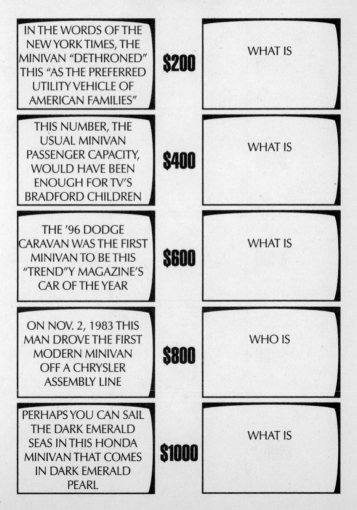

IN THE WORDS OF THE NEW YORK TIMES, THE MINIVAN "DETHRONED" THIS "AS THE PREFERRED UTILITY VEHICLE OF AMERICAN FAMILIES"	**$200**	WHAT IS
THIS NUMBER, THE USUAL MINIVAN PASSENGER CAPACITY, WOULD HAVE BEEN ENOUGH FOR TV'S BRADFORD CHILDREN	**$400**	WHAT IS
THE '96 DODGE CARAVAN WAS THE FIRST MINIVAN TO BE THIS "TREND"Y MAGAZINE'S CAR OF THE YEAR	**$600**	WHAT IS
ON NOV. 2, 1983 THIS MAN DROVE THE FIRST MODERN MINIVAN OFF A CHRYSLER ASSEMBLY LINE	**$800**	WHO IS
PERHAPS YOU CAN SAIL THE DARK EMERALD SEAS IN THIS HONDA MINIVAN THAT COMES IN DARK EMERALD PEARL	**$1000**	WHAT IS

DOUBLE JEOPARDY!

MINIVANS

$200 — WHAT IS THE STATION WAGON? — $200

$400 — WHAT IS 8? — $400

$600 — WHAT IS MOTOR TREND? — $600

$800 — WHO IS LEE IACOCCA? — $800

$1000 — WHAT IS THE ODYSSEY? — $1000

FINAL JEOPARDY!

U.S. STATESMEN

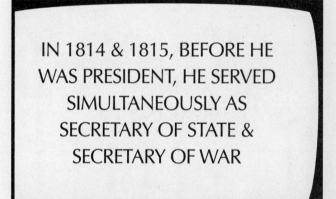

IN 1814 & 1815, BEFORE HE
WAS PRESIDENT, HE SERVED
SIMULTANEOUSLY AS
SECRETARY OF STATE &
SECRETARY OF WAR

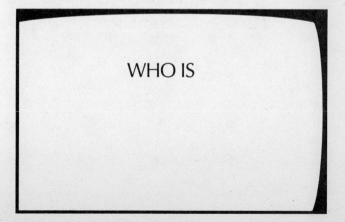

WHO IS

FINAL JEOPARDY!

U.S. STATESMEN

WHO IS
JAMES MONROE?

JEOPARDY!

MYTHS & MISSES

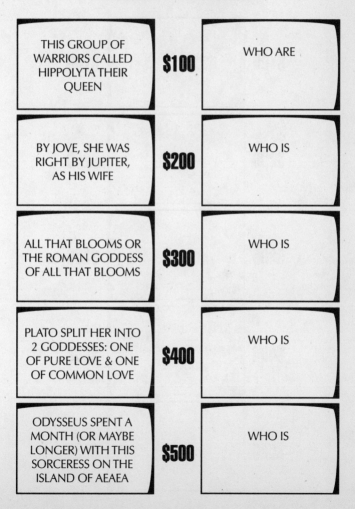

THIS GROUP OF WARRIORS CALLED HIPPOLYTA THEIR QUEEN	**$100**	WHO ARE
BY JOVE, SHE WAS RIGHT BY JUPITER, AS HIS WIFE	**$200**	WHO IS
ALL THAT BLOOMS OR THE ROMAN GODDESS OF ALL THAT BLOOMS	**$300**	WHO IS
PLATO SPLIT HER INTO 2 GODDESSES: ONE OF PURE LOVE & ONE OF COMMON LOVE	**$400**	WHO IS
ODYSSEUS SPENT A MONTH (OR MAYBE LONGER) WITH THIS SORCERESS ON THE ISLAND OF AEAEA	**$500**	WHO IS

JEOPARDY!™

MYTHS & MISSES

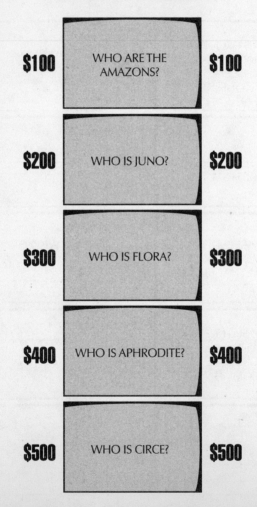

$100 · WHO ARE THE AMAZONS? · $100

$200 · WHO IS JUNO? · $200

$300 · WHO IS FLORA? · $300

$400 · WHO IS APHRODITE? · $400

$500 · WHO IS CIRCE? · $500

JEOPARDY!

CHILDREN'S GAMES

YOU CAN PUT YOUR HANDS ON YOUR HEAD ONLY IF THIS PERSON "SAYS" THAT YOU CAN	$100	WHAT IS
PIECE OF EQUIPMENT YOU NEED TO PARTICIPATE IN A DOUBLE DUTCH TOURNAMENT	$200	WHAT IS
IT'S WHAT KIDS DO WITH THEIR HANDS WHILE RECITING, "MISS MARY, MACK, MACK, MACK, ALL DRESSED IN BLACK, BLACK, BLACK . . ."	$300	WHAT IS
AN EARLY FORM OF THIS PICK-UP GAME USED KNUCKLEBONES	$400	WHAT IS
IN THIS GAME THE SHOOTER MUST KNUCKLE DOWN WITH HIS GLASSIES	$500	WHAT IS

JEOPARDY!

CHILDREN'S GAMES

$100 — WHO IS SIMON? — **$100**

$200 — WHAT IS A (JUMP) ROPE? — **$200**

$300 — WHAT IS CLAP THEM? — **$300**

$400 — WHAT IS JACKS? — **$400**

$500 — WHAT IS MARBLES? — **$500**

JEOPARDY!

STARS

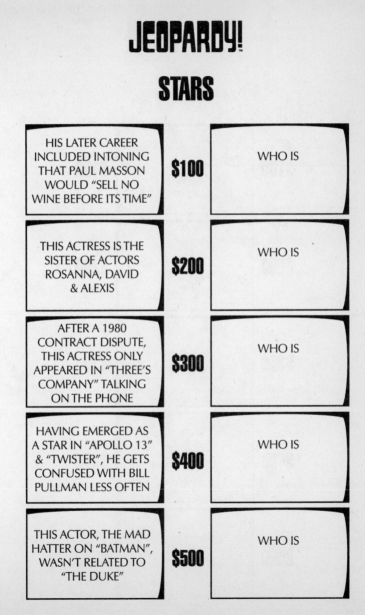

HIS LATER CAREER INCLUDED INTONING THAT PAUL MASSON WOULD "SELL NO WINE BEFORE ITS TIME"	$100	WHO IS
THIS ACTRESS IS THE SISTER OF ACTORS ROSANNA, DAVID & ALEXIS	$200	WHO IS
AFTER A 1980 CONTRACT DISPUTE, THIS ACTRESS ONLY APPEARED IN "THREE'S COMPANY" TALKING ON THE PHONE	$300	WHO IS
HAVING EMERGED AS A STAR IN "APOLLO 13" & "TWISTER", HE GETS CONFUSED WITH BILL PULLMAN LESS OFTEN	$400	WHO IS
THIS ACTOR, THE MAD HATTER ON "BATMAN", WASN'T RELATED TO "THE DUKE"	$500	WHO IS

JEOPARDY!

STARS

$100   WHO IS ORSON WELLES? $100

$200   WHO IS PATRICIA ARQUETTE? $200

$300   WHO IS SUZANNE SOMERS? $300

$400   WHO IS BILL PAXTON? $400

$500   WHO IS DAVID WAYNE? $500

JEOPARDY!™

PHYSICAL SCIENCE

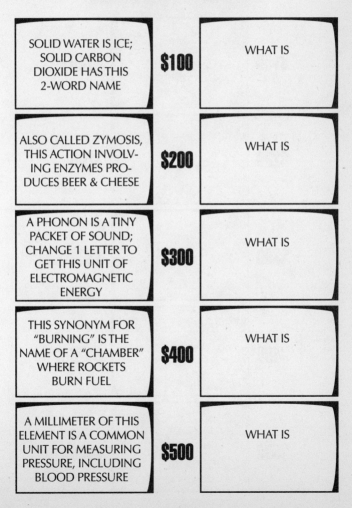

SOLID WATER IS ICE; SOLID CARBON DIOXIDE HAS THIS 2-WORD NAME	$100	WHAT IS
ALSO CALLED ZYMOSIS, THIS ACTION INVOLVING ENZYMES PRODUCES BEER & CHEESE	$200	WHAT IS
A PHONON IS A TINY PACKET OF SOUND; CHANGE 1 LETTER TO GET THIS UNIT OF ELECTROMAGNETIC ENERGY	$300	WHAT IS
THIS SYNONYM FOR "BURNING" IS THE NAME OF A "CHAMBER" WHERE ROCKETS BURN FUEL	$400	WHAT IS
A MILLIMETER OF THIS ELEMENT IS A COMMON UNIT FOR MEASURING PRESSURE, INCLUDING BLOOD PRESSURE	$500	WHAT IS

JEOPARDY!

PHYSICAL SCIENCE

$100 WHAT IS DRY ICE? **$100**

$200 WHAT IS FERMENTATION? **$200**

$300 WHAT IS A PHOTON? **$300**

$400 WHAT IS COMBUSTION? **$400**

$500 WHAT IS MERCURY? **$500**

JEOPARDY!

GANGSTER'S DICTIONARY

Clue	Value	Response
I HATES IT WHEN THE COPS PUTS THESE "BRACELETS" ON ME AFTER A BUST	$100	WHAT ARE
YOU MUGS, I NEEDS A "CAN OPENER", A TOOL USED TO OPEN ONE OF THESE, NOT A TIN CAN	$200	WHAT IS
ROLL OUT THESE "BONES", BOYS, SO WE CAN PLAY SOME GAMES OF CHANCE	$300	WHAT ARE
ONE DAY I MIGHT GO LEGIT & GET A CUSH JOB AS A "GUMSHOE", A PRIVATE ONE OF THESE	$400	WHAT IS
KEEP YOUR HEAD LOW ... I JUST SAW A "SALT & PEPPER", ONE OF THESE, GO BY	$500	WHAT IS

JEOPARDY!

GANGSTER'S DICTIONARY

$100 WHAT ARE HANDCUFFS? $100

$200 WHAT IS A SAFE? $200

$300 WHAT ARE DICE? $300

$400 WHAT IS A DETECTIVE? $400

$500 WHAT IS A POLICE CAR? $500

JEOPARDY!

THE '60s

THIS AMERICAN WENT INTO SPACE BEFORE KENNEDY MADE HIS "LET'S PUT A MAN ON THE MOON" SPEECH	**$100**	WHO IS
LACK OF PUBLIC DEMAND LED THE U.S. TREASURY TO OFFICIALLY DIS-CONTINUE THESE BILLS AUGUST 10, 1966	**$200**	WHAT ARE
SWORN IN MARCH 17, 1969, SHE SAID SHE'D PUSH FOR FACE-TO-FACE TALKS WITH THE ARABS	**$300**	WHO IS
MARTIN LUTHER KING JR.'S FREEDOM WALK IN 1965 SPANNED THE 50 MILES BETWEEN THESE 2 ALABAMA CITIES	**$400**	WHAT ARE
IN FEBRUARY 1960 A MEMBER OF THIS BREWING FAMILY WAS KIDNAPPED IN COLORADO	**$500**	WHAT IS

JEOPARDY!

THE '60s

$100   WHO IS ALAN SHEPARD (JR.)?   **$100**

$200   WHAT ARE $2 BILLS?   **$200**

$300   WHO IS GOLDA MEIR?   **$300**

$400   WHAT ARE SELMA & MONTGOMERY?   **$400**

$500   WHAT IS THE COORS FAMILY?   **$500**

DOUBLE JEOPARDY!

OXYMORONS

NAME OF A MOTOR-CYCLE GANG FOUNDED IN CALIFORNIA IN 1948; WHAT DO THEIR WINGS LOOK LIKE?	**$200**	WHAT ARE
PSYCHOLOGISTS PUT IT BEFORE "AGGRESSIVE" TO DESCRIBE BEHAVIOR LIKE SULKING & PROCRASTINATION	**$400**	WHAT IS
"SAME" THIS IS A SLANGY RESPONSE ON BEING GIVEN IRRELE-VANT INFORMATION	**$600**	WHAT IS
FRENCH KING HENRY IV CALLED ENGLISH KING JAMES I "THE WISEST" ONE OF THESE "IN CHRISTENDOM"	**$800**	WHAT IS
SHH! A 1994 SHORT STORY COLLECTION BY ALICE MUNRO IS TITLED "OPEN" THESE	**$1000**	WHAT ARE

DOUBLE JEOPARDY!

OXYMORONS

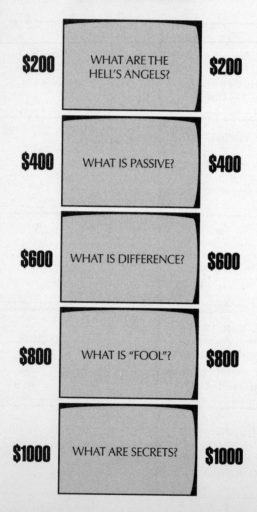

$200 — WHAT ARE THE HELL'S ANGELS? — $200

$400 — WHAT IS PASSIVE? — $400

$600 — WHAT IS DIFFERENCE? — $600

$800 — WHAT IS "FOOL"? — $800

$1000 — WHAT ARE SECRETS? — $1000

DOUBLE JEOPARDY!

GEOGRAPHY

THIS COUNTRY'S LONGEST FJORD, SOGNE FJORD, EXTENDS 127 MILES INLAND	**$200**	WHAT IS
CAPE BABA, THE WESTERNMOST POINT OF THIS CONTINENT, JUTS INTO THE AEGEAN SEA	**$400**	WHAT IS
THE SEINE RIVER RISES ON THE PLATEAU OF LANGRES NEAR THIS MUSTARD CAPITAL	**$600**	WHAT IS
IN 1610 THE DUTCH EAST INDIA COMPANY BUILT A TRADING POST IN THIS CITY; 9 YEARS LATER THEY NAMED IT BATAVIA	**$800**	WHAT IS
THIS COUNTRY'S DECCAN PLATEAU LIES BETWEEN THE EASTERN & WESTERN GHATS RANGES	**$1000**	WHAT IS

DOUBLE JEOPARDY!

GEOGRAPHY

$200 · WHAT IS NORWAY? · $200

$400 · WHAT IS ASIA? · $400

$600 · WHAT IS DIJON? · $600

$800 · WHAT IS JAKARTA? · $800

$1000 · WHAT IS INDIA? · $1000

DOUBLE JEOPARDY!

RAILROAD TERMS

Clue	Value	Response
THE PERSON IN THIS POST SUPERVISES THE TRAIN CREW & COLLECTS FARES	$200	WHAT IS
THIS TERM FOR PORTERS CAME FROM THEIR COLORFUL HEADGEAR	$400	WHAT ARE
IT'S A FIREBOX FEEDER, AN APPRENTICE TO THE ENGINEER, OR A FAMOUS BRAM	$600	WHAT IS
A TRACK INSPECTOR, WHETHER OR NOT HE'S FROM WICHITA	$800	WHAT IS
A PIN PULLER OPERATES THESE IN THE YARD, TO SHUNT CARS FROM ONE TRACK TO ANOTHER	$1000	WHAT ARE

DOUBLE JEOPARDY!

RAILROAD TERMS

$200 · WHAT IS THE CONDUCTOR? · $200

$400 · WHAT ARE REDCAPS? · $400

$600 · WHAT IS A STOKER? · $600

$800 · WHAT IS A LINEMAN? · $800

$1000 · WHAT ARE SWITCHES? · $1000

174

DOUBLE JEOPARDY!

THEATRE

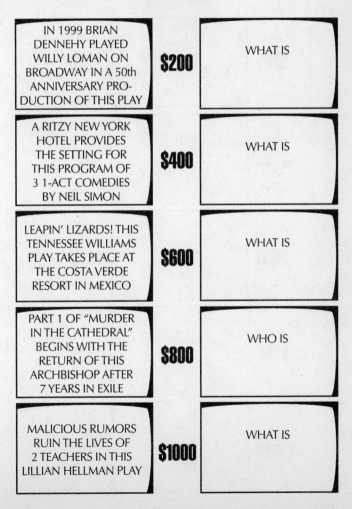

IN 1999 BRIAN DENNEHY PLAYED WILLY LOMAN ON BROADWAY IN A 50th ANNIVERSARY PRODUCTION OF THIS PLAY	**$200**	WHAT IS
A RITZY NEW YORK HOTEL PROVIDES THE SETTING FOR THIS PROGRAM OF 3 1-ACT COMEDIES BY NEIL SIMON	**$400**	WHAT IS
LEAPIN' LIZARDS! THIS TENNESSEE WILLIAMS PLAY TAKES PLACE AT THE COSTA VERDE RESORT IN MEXICO	**$600**	WHAT IS
PART 1 OF "MURDER IN THE CATHEDRAL" BEGINS WITH THE RETURN OF THIS ARCHBISHOP AFTER 7 YEARS IN EXILE	**$800**	WHO IS
MALICIOUS RUMORS RUIN THE LIVES OF 2 TEACHERS IN THIS LILLIAN HELLMAN PLAY	**$1000**	WHAT IS

DOUBLE JEOPARDY!

THEATRE

$200 — WHAT IS "DEATH OF A SALESMAN"? — $200

$400 — WHAT IS "PLAZA SUITE"? — $400

$600 — WHAT IS "THE NIGHT OF THE IGUANA"? — $600

$800 — WHO IS THOMAS (A) BECKET? — $800

$1000 — WHAT IS "THE CHILDREN'S HOUR"? — $1000

DOUBLE JEOPARDY!

SPORTS

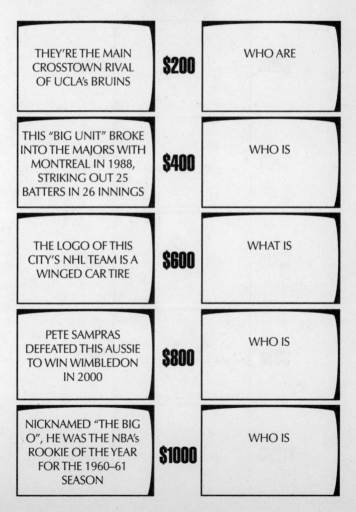

Clue	Value	Response
THEY'RE THE MAIN CROSSTOWN RIVAL OF UCLA's BRUINS	$200	WHO ARE
THIS "BIG UNIT" BROKE INTO THE MAJORS WITH MONTREAL IN 1988, STRIKING OUT 25 BATTERS IN 26 INNINGS	$400	WHO IS
THE LOGO OF THIS CITY'S NHL TEAM IS A WINGED CAR TIRE	$600	WHAT IS
PETE SAMPRAS DEFEATED THIS AUSSIE TO WIN WIMBLEDON IN 2000	$800	WHO IS
NICKNAMED "THE BIG O", HE WAS THE NBA's ROOKIE OF THE YEAR FOR THE 1960–61 SEASON	$1000	WHO IS

DOUBLE JEOPARDY!

SPORTS

$200	WHO ARE THE USC TROJANS?	$200
$400	WHO IS RANDY JOHNSON?	$400
$600	WHAT IS DETROIT?	$600
$800	WHO IS PATRICK RAFTER?	$800
$1000	WHO IS OSCAR ROBERTSON?	$1000

DOUBLE JEOPARDY!

THE BIRTH OF WORDS

Clue	Value	Response
THIS SCOTTISH ENTREE MAY DERIVE ITS NAME FROM THE OLD FRENCH HAGUIER, "TO CHOP"	**$200**	WHAT IS
POSSIBLY FROM THE LATIN FOR "FAREWELL TO MEAT", IT'S A TIME OF PRE-LENTEN MERRYMAKING	**$400**	WHAT IS
THIS TERM FOR A STEAMING HOT SPRING COMES FROM THE NAME OF A FAMOUS ICE-LANDIC HOT SPRING	**$600**	WHAT IS
FROM THE OLD SLAVIC FOR "SLAVE", THIS WORD ENTERED THE LANGUAGE FROM KAREL CAPEK'S 1921 PLAY "R.U.R."	**$800**	WHAT IS
THIS ITALIAN-SOUNDING NAME FOR A SEDUCER COMES FROM THE 1703 PLAY "THE FAIR PENITENT"	**$1000**	WHAT IS

DOUBLE JEOPARDY!

THE BIRTH OF WORDS

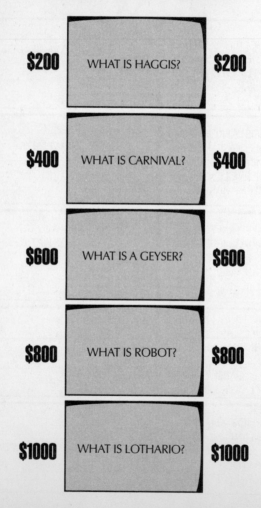

$200	WHAT IS HAGGIS?	$200
$400	WHAT IS CARNIVAL?	$400
$600	WHAT IS A GEYSER?	$600
$800	WHAT IS ROBOT?	$800
$1000	WHAT IS LOTHARIO?	$1000

FINAL JEOPARDY!
U.S. GOVERNMENT

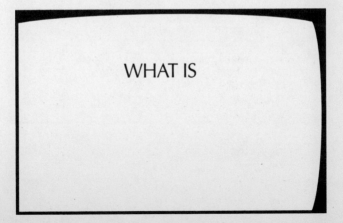

LAWRENCE WALSH &
DONALD SMALTZ
HELD THIS JOB CREATED
BY 1978's ETHICS IN
GOVERNMENT ACT

WHAT IS

FINAL JEOPARDY!

U.S. GOVERNMENT

WHAT IS
INDEPENDENT COUNSEL
OR SPECIAL PROSECUTOR?

JEOPARDY!

SUMMER

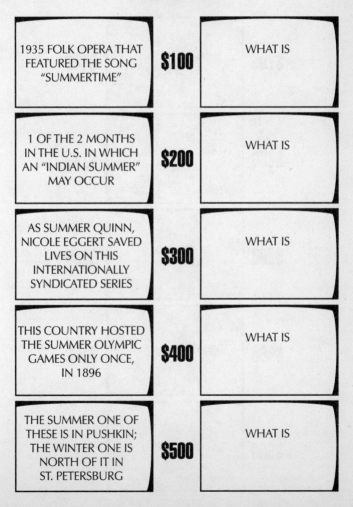

Clue	Value	Response
1935 FOLK OPERA THAT FEATURED THE SONG "SUMMERTIME"	$100	WHAT IS
1 OF THE 2 MONTHS IN THE U.S. IN WHICH AN "INDIAN SUMMER" MAY OCCUR	$200	WHAT IS
AS SUMMER QUINN, NICOLE EGGERT SAVED LIVES ON THIS INTERNATIONALLY SYNDICATED SERIES	$300	WHAT IS
THIS COUNTRY HOSTED THE SUMMER OLYMPIC GAMES ONLY ONCE, IN 1896	$400	WHAT IS
THE SUMMER ONE OF THESE IS IN PUSHKIN; THE WINTER ONE IS NORTH OF IT IN ST. PETERSBURG	$500	WHAT IS

JEOPARDY!

SUMMER

$100	WHAT IS "PORGY AND BESS"?	**$100**
$200	WHAT IS OCTOBER OR NOVEMBER?	**$200**
$300	WHAT IS "BAYWATCH"?	**$300**
$400	WHAT IS GREECE?	**$400**
$500	WHAT IS A PALACE?	**$500**

184

JEOPARDY!

WORLDLY WISDOM

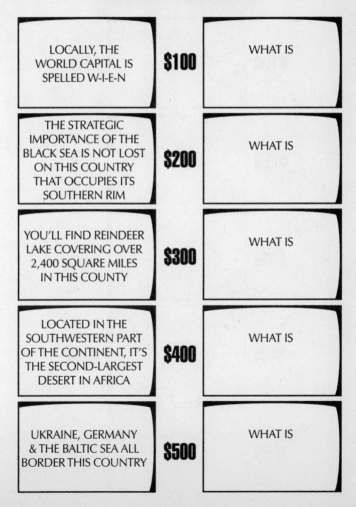

LOCALLY, THE WORLD CAPITAL IS SPELLED W-I-E-N	$100	WHAT IS
THE STRATEGIC IMPORTANCE OF THE BLACK SEA IS NOT LOST ON THIS COUNTRY THAT OCCUPIES ITS SOUTHERN RIM	$200	WHAT IS
YOU'LL FIND REINDEER LAKE COVERING OVER 2,400 SQUARE MILES IN THIS COUNTY	$300	WHAT IS
LOCATED IN THE SOUTHWESTERN PART OF THE CONTINENT, IT'S THE SECOND-LARGEST DESERT IN AFRICA	$400	WHAT IS
UKRAINE, GERMANY & THE BALTIC SEA ALL BORDER THIS COUNTRY	$500	WHAT IS

JEOPARDY!

WORLDLY WISDOM

$100 WHAT IS VIENNA? **$100**

$200 WHAT IS TURKEY? **$200**

$300 WHAT IS CANADA? **$300**

$400 WHAT IS THE KALAHARI? **$400**

$500 WHAT IS POLAND? **$500**

JEOPARDY!

WE LOVE LUCY

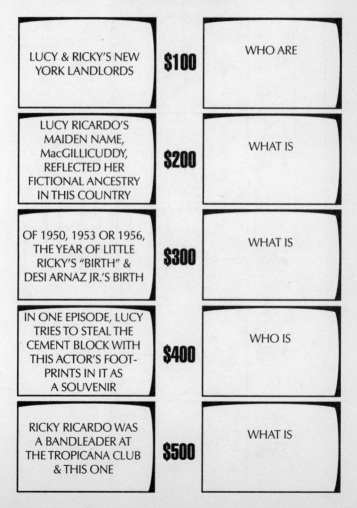

CLUE	VALUE	RESPONSE
LUCY & RICKY'S NEW YORK LANDLORDS	$100	WHO ARE
LUCY RICARDO'S MAIDEN NAME, MacGILLICUDDY, REFLECTED HER FICTIONAL ANCESTRY IN THIS COUNTRY	$200	WHAT IS
OF 1950, 1953 OR 1956, THE YEAR OF LITTLE RICKY'S "BIRTH" & DESI ARNAZ JR.'S BIRTH	$300	WHAT IS
IN ONE EPISODE, LUCY TRIES TO STEAL THE CEMENT BLOCK WITH THIS ACTOR'S FOOTPRINTS IN IT AS A SOUVENIR	$400	WHO IS
RICKY RICARDO WAS A BANDLEADER AT THE TROPICANA CLUB & THIS ONE	$500	WHAT IS

JEOPARDY!™

WE LOVE LUCY

$100 WHO ARE FRED & ETHEL MERTZ? $100

$200 WHAT IS SCOTLAND? $200

$300 WHAT IS 1953? $300

$400 WHO IS JOHN WAYNE? $400

$500 WHAT IS THE BABALU CLUB? $500

JEOPARDY!

THE ANIMAL KINGDOM

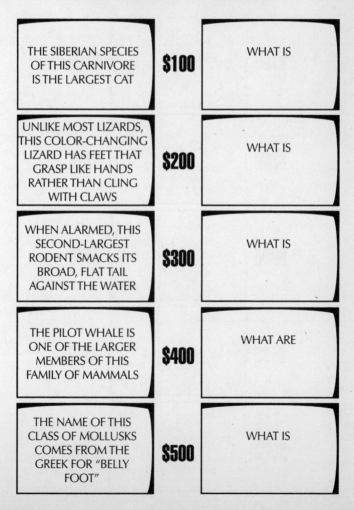

THE SIBERIAN SPECIES OF THIS CARNIVORE IS THE LARGEST CAT	**$100**	WHAT IS
UNLIKE MOST LIZARDS, THIS COLOR-CHANGING LIZARD HAS FEET THAT GRASP LIKE HANDS RATHER THAN CLING WITH CLAWS	**$200**	WHAT IS
WHEN ALARMED, THIS SECOND-LARGEST RODENT SMACKS ITS BROAD, FLAT TAIL AGAINST THE WATER	**$300**	WHAT IS
THE PILOT WHALE IS ONE OF THE LARGER MEMBERS OF THIS FAMILY OF MAMMALS	**$400**	WHAT ARE
THE NAME OF THIS CLASS OF MOLLUSKS COMES FROM THE GREEK FOR "BELLY FOOT"	**$500**	WHAT IS

JEOPARDY!

THE ANIMAL KINGDOM

$100 WHAT IS THE TIGER? **$100**

$200 WHAT IS THE CHAMELEON? **$200**

$300 WHAT IS THE BEAVER? **$300**

$400 WHAT ARE DOLPHINS? **$400**

$500 WHAT IS GASTROPODA? **$500**

JEOPARDY!™

THE NAME'S FAMILIAR

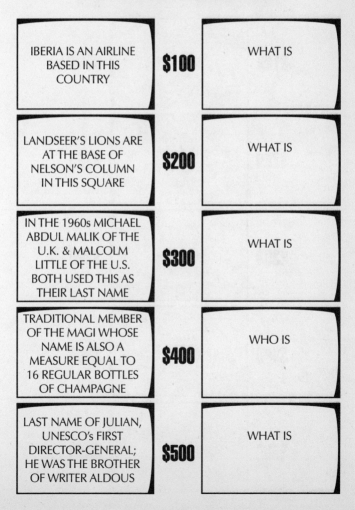

Clue	Value	Response
IBERIA IS AN AIRLINE BASED IN THIS COUNTRY	$100	WHAT IS
LANDSEER'S LIONS ARE AT THE BASE OF NELSON'S COLUMN IN THIS SQUARE	$200	WHAT IS
IN THE 1960s MICHAEL ABDUL MALIK OF THE U.K. & MALCOLM LITTLE OF THE U.S. BOTH USED THIS AS THEIR LAST NAME	$300	WHAT IS
TRADITIONAL MEMBER OF THE MAGI WHOSE NAME IS ALSO A MEASURE EQUAL TO 16 REGULAR BOTTLES OF CHAMPAGNE	$400	WHO IS
LAST NAME OF JULIAN, UNESCO's FIRST DIRECTOR-GENERAL; HE WAS THE BROTHER OF WRITER ALDOUS	$500	WHAT IS

JEOPARDY!

THE NAME'S FAMILIAR

$100   WHAT IS SPAIN? $100

$200   WHAT IS TRAFALGAR SQUARE? $200

$300   WHAT IS X? $300

$400   WHO IS BALTHAZAR? $400

$500   WHAT IS HUXLEY? $500

JEOPARDY!

"BOR"ING

Clue	Value	Response
A RECENT CONVERT TO CHRISTIANITY OR ONE WITH A RENEWED FAITH IS DESCRIBED AS THIS	$100	WHAT IS
YOU'LL FIND THE MEDOC, SAUTERNES & SOME GRAND CHATEAUX IN THIS REGION OF FRANCE	$200	WHAT IS
THIS TERM FOR A HOUSE OF ILL REPUTE GOES BACK TO THE 16th CENTURY	$300	WHAT IS
ISLAND IN THE SOUTH CHINA SEA ON WHICH YOU'D FIND BRUNEI & PART OF INDONESIA	$400	WHAT IS
HE CIRCLED THE EARTH IN 1965 & CIRCLED THE MOON IN 1968	$500	WHO IS

JEOPARDY!

"BOR"ING

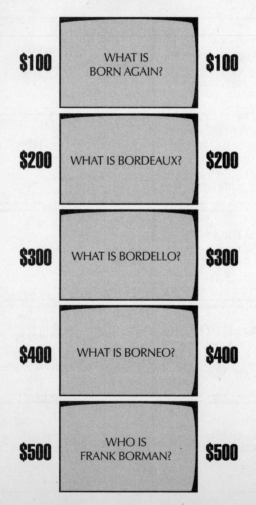

$100 — WHAT IS BORN AGAIN? — $100

$200 — WHAT IS BORDEAUX? — $200

$300 — WHAT IS BORDELLO? — $300

$400 — WHAT IS BORNEO? — $400

$500 — WHO IS FRANK BORMAN? — $500

DOUBLE JEOPARDY!

CLASSICAL COMPOSERS

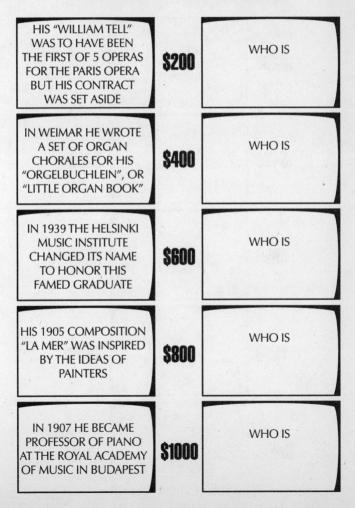

HIS "WILLIAM TELL" WAS TO HAVE BEEN THE FIRST OF 5 OPERAS FOR THE PARIS OPERA BUT HIS CONTRACT WAS SET ASIDE	$200	WHO IS
IN WEIMAR HE WROTE A SET OF ORGAN CHORALES FOR HIS "ORGELBUCHLEIN", OR "LITTLE ORGAN BOOK"	$400	WHO IS
IN 1939 THE HELSINKI MUSIC INSTITUTE CHANGED ITS NAME TO HONOR THIS FAMED GRADUATE	$600	WHO IS
HIS 1905 COMPOSITION "LA MER" WAS INSPIRED BY THE IDEAS OF PAINTERS	$800	WHO IS
IN 1907 HE BECAME PROFESSOR OF PIANO AT THE ROYAL ACADEMY OF MUSIC IN BUDAPEST	$1000	WHO IS

DOUBLE JEOPARDY!

CLASSICAL COMPOSERS

$200 · WHO IS GIOACCHINO ROSSINI? · $200

$400 · WHO IS JOHANN SEBASTIAN BACH? · $400

$600 · WHO IS JEAN SIBELIUS? · $600

$800 · WHO IS CLAUDE DEBUSSY? · $800

$1000 · WHO IS BELA BARTOK? · $1000

DOUBLE JEOPARDY!

FOOD

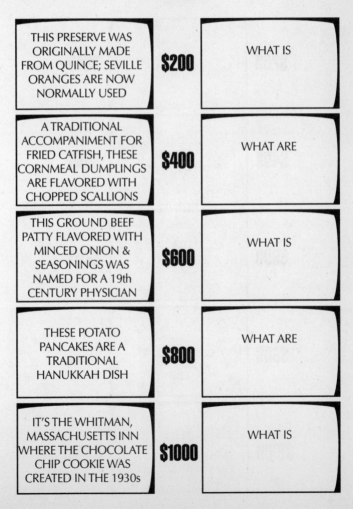

THIS PRESERVE WAS ORIGINALLY MADE FROM QUINCE; SEVILLE ORANGES ARE NOW NORMALLY USED	**$200**	WHAT IS
A TRADITIONAL ACCOMPANIMENT FOR FRIED CATFISH, THESE CORNMEAL DUMPLINGS ARE FLAVORED WITH CHOPPED SCALLIONS	**$400**	WHAT ARE
THIS GROUND BEEF PATTY FLAVORED WITH MINCED ONION & SEASONINGS WAS NAMED FOR A 19th CENTURY PHYSICIAN	**$600**	WHAT IS
THESE POTATO PANCAKES ARE A TRADITIONAL HANUKKAH DISH	**$800**	WHAT ARE
IT'S THE WHITMAN, MASSACHUSETTS INN WHERE THE CHOCOLATE CHIP COOKIE WAS CREATED IN THE 1930s	**$1000**	WHAT IS

DOUBLE JEOPARDY!

FOOD

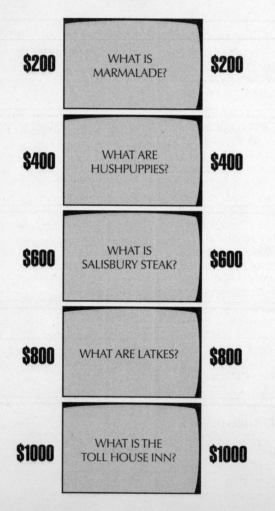

$200	WHAT IS MARMALADE?	**$200**
$400	WHAT ARE HUSHPUPPIES?	**$400**
$600	WHAT IS SALISBURY STEAK?	**$600**
$800	WHAT ARE LATKES?	**$800**
$1000	WHAT IS THE TOLL HOUSE INN?	**$1000**

DOUBLE JEOPARDY!

MEDICAL ABBREV.

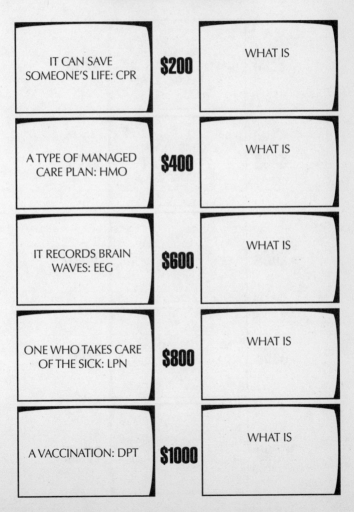

IT CAN SAVE SOMEONE'S LIFE: CPR	**$200**	WHAT IS
A TYPE OF MANAGED CARE PLAN: HMO	**$400**	WHAT IS
IT RECORDS BRAIN WAVES: EEG	**$600**	WHAT IS
ONE WHO TAKES CARE OF THE SICK: LPN	**$800**	WHAT IS
A VACCINATION: DPT	**$1000**	WHAT IS

DOUBLE JEOPARDY!

MEDICAL ABBREV.

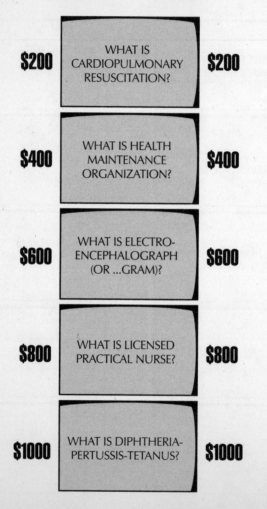

$200 — WHAT IS CARDIOPULMONARY RESUSCITATION? — **$200**

$400 — WHAT IS HEALTH MAINTENANCE ORGANIZATION? — **$400**

$600 — WHAT IS ELECTRO-ENCEPHALOGRAPH (OR ...GRAM)? — **$600**

$800 — WHAT IS LICENSED PRACTICAL NURSE? — **$800**

$1000 — WHAT IS DIPHTHERIA-PERTUSSIS-TETANUS? — **$1000**

DOUBLE JEOPARDY!

DIRECTORS & FILMS

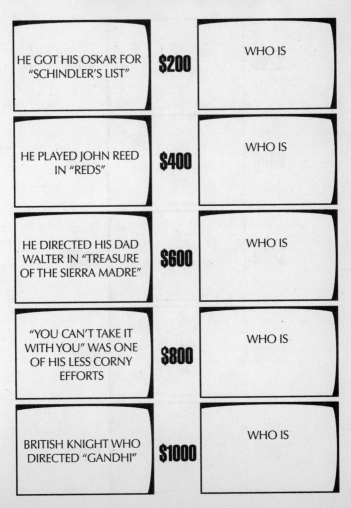

Clue	Value	Response
HE GOT HIS OSKAR FOR "SCHINDLER'S LIST"	$200	WHO IS
HE PLAYED JOHN REED IN "REDS"	$400	WHO IS
HE DIRECTED HIS DAD WALTER IN "TREASURE OF THE SIERRA MADRE"	$600	WHO IS
"YOU CAN'T TAKE IT WITH YOU" WAS ONE OF HIS LESS CORNY EFFORTS	$800	WHO IS
BRITISH KNIGHT WHO DIRECTED "GANDHI"	$1000	WHO IS

DOUBLE JEOPARDY!

DIRECTORS & FILMS

$200 — WHO IS STEVEN SPIELBERG? — $200

$400 — WHO IS WARREN BEATTY? — $400

$600 — WHO IS JOHN HUSTON? — $600

$800 — WHO IS FRANK CAPRA? — $800

$1000 — WHO IS (SIR) RICHARD ATTENBOROUGH? — $1000

DOUBLE JEOPARDY!

GOING DUTCH

IN HER DIARY SHE WROTE, "IT IS NOT THE DUTCH PEOPLE'S FAULT THAT WE ARE HAVING SUCH A MISERABLE TIME"	**$200**	WHO IS
JOHAN CRUYFF, KNOWN AS THE DUTCH MASTER, WAS TOPS IN THIS SPORT & EVEN PLAYED FOR THE L.A. AZTECS	**$400**	WHAT IS
IN 1993 NORTHWEST AIRLINES FORMED AN ALLIANCE WITH THIS DUTCH COMPANY	**$600**	WHAT IS
THE ROOTS OF THIS U.S. STATE CAPITAL GO BACK TO FORT NASSAU, A TRADING POST FOUNDED BY THE DUTCH IN 1614	**$800**	WHAT IS
A NEW WATERWAY OPENED IN 1872 ALLOWED LARGE VESSELS PASSAGE TO THIS DUTCH CITY, NOW A TOP WORLD PORT	**$1000**	WHAT IS

DOUBLE JEOPARDY!

GOING DUTCH

$200 WHO IS ANNE FRANK? **$200**

$400 WHAT IS SOCCER? **$400**

$600 WHAT IS KLM (ROYAL DUTCH AIRLINES)? **$600**

$800 WHAT IS ALBANY (NEW YORK)? **$800**

$1000 WHAT IS ROTTERDAM? **$1000**

DOUBLE JEOPARDY!

WHICH CAME FIRST?

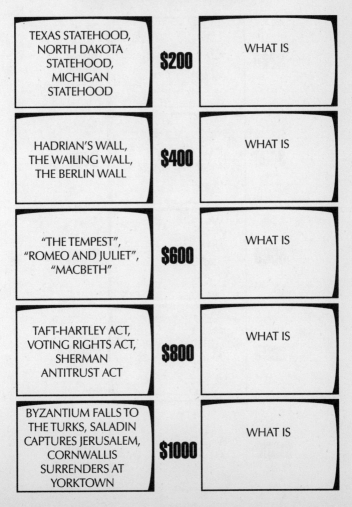

TEXAS STATEHOOD, NORTH DAKOTA STATEHOOD, MICHIGAN STATEHOOD	$200	WHAT IS
HADRIAN'S WALL, THE WAILING WALL, THE BERLIN WALL	$400	WHAT IS
"THE TEMPEST", "ROMEO AND JULIET", "MACBETH"	$600	WHAT IS
TAFT-HARTLEY ACT, VOTING RIGHTS ACT, SHERMAN ANTITRUST ACT	$800	WHAT IS
BYZANTIUM FALLS TO THE TURKS, SALADIN CAPTURES JERUSALEM, CORNWALLIS SURRENDERS AT YORKTOWN	$1000	WHAT IS

DOUBLE JEOPARDY!

WHICH CAME FIRST?

$200

WHAT IS MICHIGAN STATEHOOD?

$200

$400

WHAT IS THE WAILING WALL?

$400

$600

WHAT IS "ROMEO AND JULIET"?

$600

$800

WHAT IS THE SHERMAN ANTITRUST ACT?

$800

$1000

WHAT IS SALADIN CAPTURES JERUSALEM?

$1000

FINAL JEOPARDY!

QUOTABLE DEFINITIONS

TED HUGHES WROTE THAT
IT'S WHERE A CHILD CAN
SIT "WITH THE GENIUS
OF THE EARTH"

WHERE IS

FINAL JEOPARDY!

QUOTABLE DEFINITIONS

WHERE IS
IN THE LIBRARY?

JEOPARDY!

AMERICANA

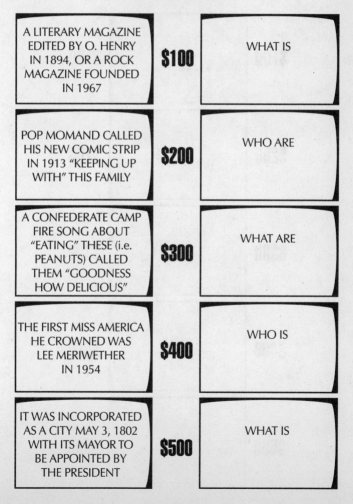

Clue	Value	Response
A LITERARY MAGAZINE EDITED BY O. HENRY IN 1894, OR A ROCK MAGAZINE FOUNDED IN 1967	$100	WHAT IS
POP MOMAND CALLED HIS NEW COMIC STRIP IN 1913 "KEEPING UP WITH" THIS FAMILY	$200	WHO ARE
A CONFEDERATE CAMP FIRE SONG ABOUT "EATING" THESE (i.e. PEANUTS) CALLED THEM "GOODNESS HOW DELICIOUS"	$300	WHAT ARE
THE FIRST MISS AMERICA HE CROWNED WAS LEE MERIWETHER IN 1954	$400	WHO IS
IT WAS INCORPORATED AS A CITY MAY 3, 1802 WITH ITS MAYOR TO BE APPOINTED BY THE PRESIDENT	$500	WHAT IS

JEOPARDY!

AMERICANA

$100	WHAT IS ROLLING STONE?	**$100**
$200	WHO ARE THE JONESES?	**$200**
$300	WHAT ARE GOOBER PEAS?	**$300**
$400	WHO IS BERT PARKS?	**$400**
$500	WHAT IS WASHINGTON, D.C.?	**$500**

JEOPARDY!

"WHIP"s & "CHAIN"s

IT'S A SERIES OF POSITIONS IN WHICH EACH ONE HAS DIRECT AUTHORITY OVER THE ONE IMMEDIATELY BELOW	$100	WHAT IS
SENATE POSITION HELD BY NEVADA DEMOCRAT HARRY REID	$200	WHAT IS
THIS NORTH AMERICAN BIRD IS NAMED FOR ITS ODD CALL, WHICH IT MAY REPEAT SEVERAL HUNDRED TIMES WITHOUT STOPPING	$300	WHAT IS
TOOL PREFERRED BY LEATHERFACE IN A 1974 HORROR CLASSIC	$400	WHAT IS
"A SANDWICH JUST ISN'T A SANDWICH WITHOUT" THE "TANGY ZIP" OF THIS KRAFT SALAD DRESSING	$500	WHAT IS

JEOPARDY!

"WHIP"s & "CHAIN"s

$100	WHAT IS CHAIN OF COMMAND?	$100
$200	WHAT IS MINORITY WHIP?	$200
$300	WHAT IS THE WHIPPOORWILL?	$300
$400	WHAT IS A CHAINSAW?	$400
$500	WHAT IS MIRACLE WHIP?	$500

JEOPARDY!

WHAT'S THE MATTER ... YELLOW??

Clue	Value	Response
APPROPRIATELY, YOU CAN SEE THE YELLOW-BELLIED MARMOT IN THIS WYOMING-MONTANA-IDAHO NATIONAL PARK	$100	WHAT IS
THE YELLOW-WINGED TYPE OF THIS MAMMAL HOPES INSECTS DON'T SEE ITS YELLOW WINGS COMING	$200	WHAT IS
CALL IT CRAZY, BUT UNLIKE OTHER TYPES OF THESE BIRDS, THE YELLOW-BILLED ONE BUILDS ITS OWN NEST INSTEAD OF INVADING	$300	WHAT IS
NARCISSUS PSEUDO-NARCISSUS IS THE SCIENTIFIC NAME OF THIS STRIKING YELLOW FLOWER	$400	WHAT IS
EAST AFRICA IS HOME TO THE YELLOW SPECIES OF THESE LARGE MONKEYS KNOWN FOR THEIR COLORFUL BOTTOMS	$500	WHAT ARE

JEOPARDY!

WHAT'S THE MATTER ... YELLOW??

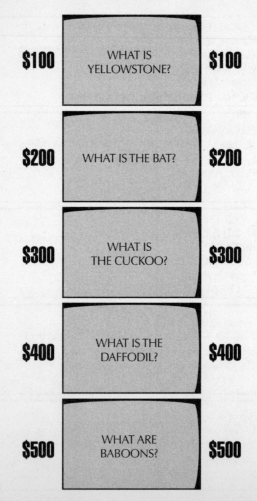

$100   WHAT IS YELLOWSTONE? $100

$200   WHAT IS THE BAT? $200

$300   WHAT IS THE CUCKOO? $300

$400   WHAT IS THE DAFFODIL? $400

$500   WHAT ARE BABOONS? $500

JEOPARDY!

PEOPLE IN HISTORY

THIS FIRST U.S. FIRST LADY, A FINE EQUESTRIENNE, ONCE RODE A HORSE UP THE STAIRS OF HER UNCLE'S HOUSE	**$100**	WHO IS
INDIA'S 5th CENTURY PLAYWRIGHT KALIDASA WROTE HIS MASTER-PIECE, "SHAKUNTALA", IN THIS CLASSICAL LANGUAGE	**$200**	WHAT IS
HE WAS CONDEMNED, BUT NOT CENSURED, BY THE SENATE IN DECEMBER 1954	**$300**	WHO IS
THE LAST KING WILLIAM TO RULE ENGLAND HAD THIS NUMBER AFTER HIS NAME	**$400**	WHAT. IS
HE WAS CHIEF MINISTER OF FRANCE FROM 1624 TO 1642	**$500**	WHO IS

215

JEOPARDY!

PEOPLE IN HISTORY

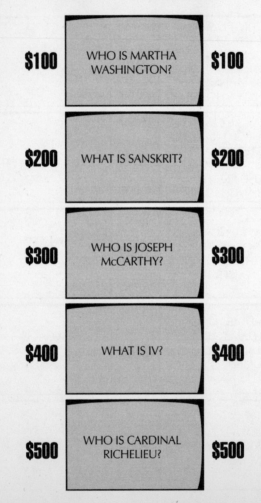

$100 — WHO IS MARTHA WASHINGTON? — $100

$200 — WHAT IS SANSKRIT? — $200

$300 — WHO IS JOSEPH McCARTHY? — $300

$400 — WHAT IS IV? — $400

$500 — WHO IS CARDINAL RICHELIEU? — $500

JEOPARDY!

LITERATURE

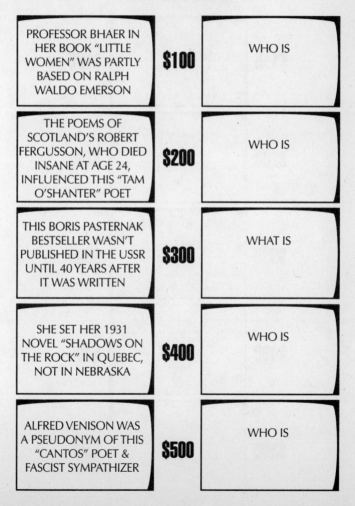

PROFESSOR BHAER IN HER BOOK "LITTLE WOMEN" WAS PARTLY BASED ON RALPH WALDO EMERSON	**$100**	WHO IS
THE POEMS OF SCOTLAND'S ROBERT FERGUSSON, WHO DIED INSANE AT AGE 24, INFLUENCED THIS "TAM O'SHANTER" POET	**$200**	WHO IS
THIS BORIS PASTERNAK BESTSELLER WASN'T PUBLISHED IN THE USSR UNTIL 40 YEARS AFTER IT WAS WRITTEN	**$300**	WHAT IS
SHE SET HER 1931 NOVEL "SHADOWS ON THE ROCK" IN QUEBEC, NOT IN NEBRASKA	**$400**	WHO IS
ALFRED VENISON WAS A PSEUDONYM OF THIS "CANTOS" POET & FASCIST SYMPATHIZER	**$500**	WHO IS

JEOPARDY!

LITERATURE

$100	WHO IS LOUISA MAY ALCOTT?	**$100**
$200	WHO IS ROBERT BURNS?	**$200**
$300	WHAT IS "DOCTOR ZHIVAGO"?	**$300**
$400	WHO IS WILLA CATHER?	**$400**
$500	WHO IS EZRA POUND?	**$500**

JEOPARDY!

DEREK JETER

IN 2000 DEREK BECAME THE FIRST YANKEE EVER NAMED MVP OF THIS ANNUAL GAME	**$100**	WHAT IS
DEREK REPORTEDLY BEGAN A ROMANCE WITH THIS CHART-TOPPING SINGER AFTER MEETING HER AT A FRESH AIR FUND EVENT	**$200**	WHO IS
IN THE YANKEES' 1998 & 1999 WORLD SERIES SWEEPS OF THESE 2 TEAMS, DEREK HIT IN ALL 8 GAMES	**$300**	WHAT ARE
DEREK WENT TO HIGH SCHOOL IN THIS MICHIGAN CITY, & PROBABLY HAD A GAL THERE; MAYBE MORE THAN ONE	**$400**	WHAT IS
DEREK'S ABOUT A YEAR YOUNGER THAN THIS RED SOX SHORTSTOP WITH WHOM HE'S OFTEN COMPARED	**$500**	WHO IS

JEOPARDY!

DEREK JETER

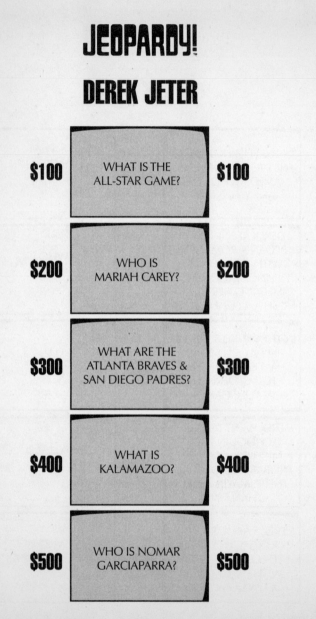

$100   WHAT IS THE ALL-STAR GAME? $100

$200   WHO IS MARIAH CAREY? $200

$300   WHAT ARE THE ATLANTA BRAVES & SAN DIEGO PADRES? $300

$400   WHAT IS KALAMAZOO? $400

$500   WHO IS NOMAR GARCIAPARRA? $500

DOUBLE JEOPARDY!

CHINA

Clue	Value	Response
THE INITIAL PHASE OF THIS LARGE BARRIER ALONG THE FRONTIER WAS COMPLETED AROUND 204 B.C.	$200	WHAT IS
ONE OF HER LAST BOOKS WAS 1972's "CHINA PAST AND PRESENT"	$400	WHO IS
THE CEDING OF HONG KONG TO GREAT BRITAIN WAS ONE RESULT OF 2 WARS NAMED FOR THIS SUBSTANCE	$600	WHAT IS
ITS PRINCIPAL TRIBUTARIES INCLUDE THE JIALING, THE MIN & THE YALONG	$800	WHAT IS
THIS MAN LED THE 1911 REVOLUTIONARY MOVEMENT DEDICATED TO ESTABLISHING DEMOCRACY IN CHINA	$1000	WHO IS

DOUBLE JEOPARDY!

CHINA

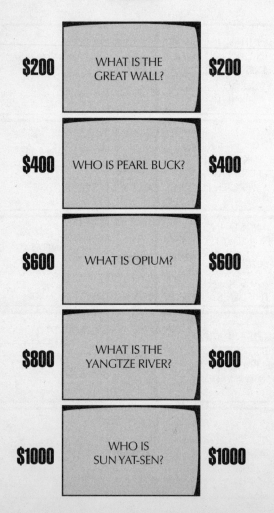

$200	WHAT IS THE GREAT WALL?	**$200**
$400	WHO IS PEARL BUCK?	**$400**
$600	WHAT IS OPIUM?	**$600**
$800	WHAT IS THE YANGTZE RIVER?	**$800**
$1000	WHO IS SUN YAT-SEN?	**$1000**

DOUBLE JEOPARDY!

WHAT A "GREAT" MOVIE!

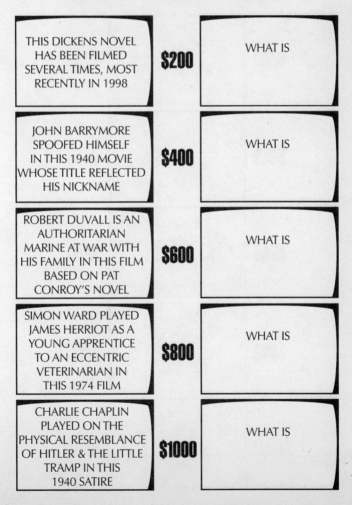

THIS DICKENS NOVEL HAS BEEN FILMED SEVERAL TIMES, MOST RECENTLY IN 1998	**$200**	WHAT IS
JOHN BARRYMORE SPOOFED HIMSELF IN THIS 1940 MOVIE WHOSE TITLE REFLECTED HIS NICKNAME	**$400**	WHAT IS
ROBERT DUVALL IS AN AUTHORITARIAN MARINE AT WAR WITH HIS FAMILY IN THIS FILM BASED ON PAT CONROY'S NOVEL	**$600**	WHAT IS
SIMON WARD PLAYED JAMES HERRIOT AS A YOUNG APPRENTICE TO AN ECCENTRIC VETERINARIAN IN THIS 1974 FILM	**$800**	WHAT IS
CHARLIE CHAPLIN PLAYED ON THE PHYSICAL RESEMBLANCE OF HITLER & THE LITTLE TRAMP IN THIS 1940 SATIRE	**$1000**	WHAT IS

DOUBLE JEOPARDY!

WHAT A "GREAT" MOVIE!

$200 — WHAT IS "GREAT EXPECTATIONS"? — **$200**

$400 — WHAT IS "THE GREAT PROFILE"? — **$400**

$600 — WHAT IS "THE GREAT SANTINI"? — **$600**

$800 — WHAT IS "ALL CREATURES GREAT AND SMALL"? — **$800**

$1000 — WHAT IS "THE GREAT DICTATOR"? — **$1000**

DOUBLE JEOPARDY!

FOREVER

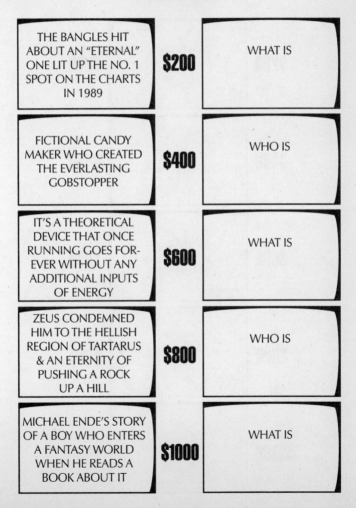

Clue	Value	Response
THE BANGLES HIT ABOUT AN "ETERNAL" ONE LIT UP THE NO. 1 SPOT ON THE CHARTS IN 1989	$200	WHAT IS
FICTIONAL CANDY MAKER WHO CREATED THE EVERLASTING GOBSTOPPER	$400	WHO IS
IT'S A THEORETICAL DEVICE THAT ONCE RUNNING GOES FOREVER WITHOUT ANY ADDITIONAL INPUTS OF ENERGY	$600	WHAT IS
ZEUS CONDEMNED HIM TO THE HELLISH REGION OF TARTARUS & AN ETERNITY OF PUSHING A ROCK UP A HILL	$800	WHO IS
MICHAEL ENDE'S STORY OF A BOY WHO ENTERS A FANTASY WORLD WHEN HE READS A BOOK ABOUT IT	$1000	WHAT IS

DOUBLE JEOPARDY!

FOREVER

$200 — WHAT IS A(N ETERNAL) FLAME? — $200

$400 — WHO IS WILLY WONKA? — $400

$600 — WHAT IS A PERPETUAL MOTION MACHINE? — $600

$800 — WHO IS SISYPHUS? — $800

$1000 — WHAT IS "THE NEVERENDING STORY"? — $1000

DOUBLE JEOPARDY!

BOOKS & AUTHORS

IN 1998 HE BROUGHT BACK EX-NAVY SEAL & FORMER CIA AGENT JOHN CLARK IN THE TECHNO-THRILLER "RAINBOW SIX"	**$200**	WHO IS
THIS JOHN GRISHAM BESTSELLER ABOUT CORRUPTION IN THE INSURANCE BUSINESS WAS TURNED INTO A 1997 FILM	**$400**	WHAT IS
HIS 1950 CLASSIC "I, ROBOT" CONTAINS 9 RELATED STORIES ABOUT (WHAT ELSE?) ROBOTS	**$600**	WHO IS
SHE WROTE ABOUT HER FATHER & "WOMEN OF COURAGE" AS WELL AS OF MURDER "IN GEORGETOWN"	**$800**	WHO IS
THIS CAMUS NOVEL IS KNOWN IN FRENCH AS "LA PESTE"	**$1000**	WHAT IS

DOUBLE JEOPARDY!

BOOKS & AUTHORS

$200   WHO IS TOM CLANCY?   **$200**

$400   WHAT IS "THE RAINMAKER"?   **$400**

$600   WHO IS ISAAC ASIMOV?   **$600**

$800   WHO IS MARGARET TRUMAN (DANIEL)?   **$800**

$1000   WHAT IS "THE PLAGUE"?   **$1000**

DOUBLE JEOPARDY!

CHARLEMAGNE

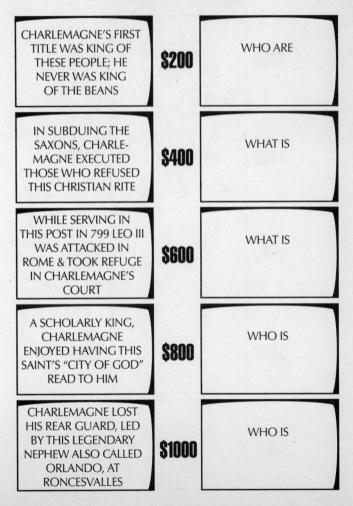

CHARLEMAGNE'S FIRST TITLE WAS KING OF THESE PEOPLE; HE NEVER WAS KING OF THE BEANS	$200	WHO ARE
IN SUBDUING THE SAXONS, CHARLEMAGNE EXECUTED THOSE WHO REFUSED THIS CHRISTIAN RITE	$400	WHAT IS
WHILE SERVING IN THIS POST IN 799 LEO III WAS ATTACKED IN ROME & TOOK REFUGE IN CHARLEMAGNE'S COURT	$600	WHAT IS
A SCHOLARLY KING, CHARLEMAGNE ENJOYED HAVING THIS SAINT'S "CITY OF GOD" READ TO HIM	$800	WHO IS
CHARLEMAGNE LOST HIS REAR GUARD, LED BY THIS LEGENDARY NEPHEW ALSO CALLED ORLANDO, AT RONCESVALLES	$1000	WHO IS

DOUBLE JEOPARDY!

CHARLEMAGNE

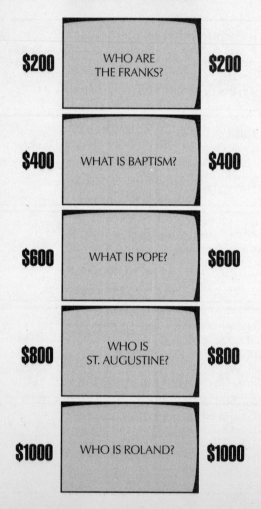

$200   WHO ARE THE FRANKS?   **$200**

$400   WHAT IS BAPTISM?   **$400**

$600   WHAT IS POPE?   **$600**

$800   WHO IS ST. AUGUSTINE?   **$800**

$1000   WHO IS ROLAND?   **$1000**

DOUBLE JEOPARDY!

FASHION STATEMENTS

IF YOU'RE DISCOVERED IN AN EMBARRASSING SITUATION, YOU'RE SAID TO BE CAUGHT "WITH" THESE "DOWN"	**$200**	WHAT ARE
WHEN YOU CONCEAL SOMETHING, YOU "DRAW" THIS BRIDAL ACCESSORY "OVER IT"	**$400**	WHAT IS
A PHRASE THAT MEANS OUTDATED, OR A DERBY YOU HAVEN'T WORN FOR DECADES	**$600**	WHAT IS
IT'S BELIEVED NAPO-LEON ORIGINATED THE PHRASE ABOUT "AN IRON HAND IN" ONE OF THESE	**$800**	WHAT IS
AS GARIBALDI'S FOLLOWERS WERE KNOWN AS REDSHIRTS, MUSSOLINI'S DEVOTEES WERE CALLED THESE	**$1000**	WHAT ARE

DOUBLE JEOPARDY!

FASHION STATEMENTS

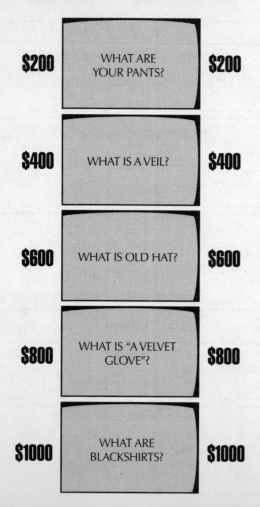

$200   WHAT ARE YOUR PANTS? $200

$400   WHAT IS A VEIL? $400

$600   WHAT IS OLD HAT? $600

$800   WHAT IS "A VELVET GLOVE"? $800

$1000   WHAT ARE BLACKSHIRTS? $1000

FINAL JEOPARDY!

CONDUCTORS

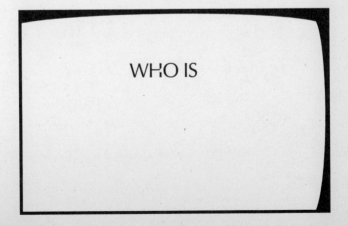

"REACHING FOR THE NOTE"
WAS THE SUBTITLE OF A
1998 FILM ABOUT THIS
AMERICAN MUSIC LEGEND
WHO DIED IN 1990

WHO IS

FINAL JEOPARDY!

CONDUCTORS

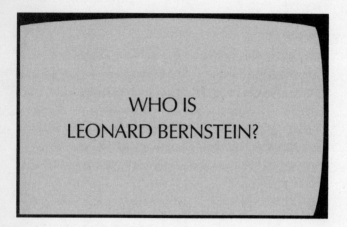

WHO IS
LEONARD BERNSTEIN?

JEOPARDY!

COUNTY SEATS

HILO, I LOVE YOU, YOU'RE THE SEAT OF THIS COUNTY THAT'S ALSO A "BIG ISLAND"	**$100**	WHAT IS
PARIS (POPULATION 8,730) IS THE SEAT OF BOURBON COUNTY IN THIS STATE	**$200**	WHAT IS
THIS IOWA CITY, THE SEAT OF BLACK HAWK COUNTRY, HAS A NAME WELLINGTON WOULD REMEMBER	**$300**	WHAT IS
QUINCY, ILLINOIS IS THE SEAT OF A COUNTY WITH THIS PRESIDENTIAL NAME	**$400**	WHAT IS
AS I WALKED OUT IN THE STREETS OF THIS CITY, I WAS IN THE SEAT OF WEBB COUNTY, TEXAS	**$500**	WHAT IS

JEOPARDY!

COUNTY SEATS

$100   WHAT IS HAWAII? $100

$200   WHAT IS KENTUCKY? $200

$300   WHAT IS WATERLOO? $300

$400   WHAT IS ADAMS? $400

$500   WHAT IS LAREDO? $500

JEOPARDY!

WEAPONS

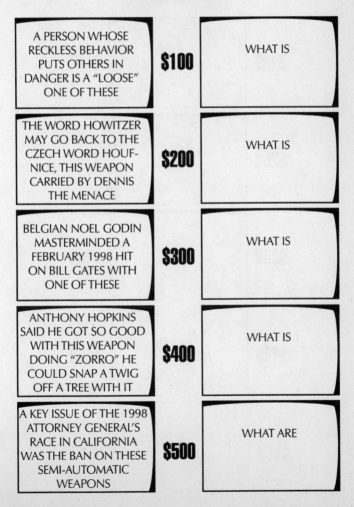

A PERSON WHOSE RECKLESS BEHAVIOR PUTS OTHERS IN DANGER IS A "LOOSE" ONE OF THESE	$100	WHAT IS
THE WORD HOWITZER MAY GO BACK TO THE CZECH WORD HOUF-NICE, THIS WEAPON CARRIED BY DENNIS THE MENACE	$200	WHAT IS
BELGIAN NOEL GODIN MASTERMINDED A FEBRUARY 1998 HIT ON BILL GATES WITH ONE OF THESE	$300	WHAT IS
ANTHONY HOPKINS SAID HE GOT SO GOOD WITH THIS WEAPON DOING "ZORRO" HE COULD SNAP A TWIG OFF A TREE WITH IT	$400	WHAT IS
A KEY ISSUE OF THE 1998 ATTORNEY GENERAL'S RACE IN CALIFORNIA WAS THE BAN ON THESE SEMI-AUTOMATIC WEAPONS	$500	WHAT ARE

JEOPARDY!

WEAPONS

$100   WHAT IS A CANNON? $100

$200   WHAT IS A SLINGSHOT? $200

$300   WHAT IS A (CREAM) PIE? $300

$400   WHAT IS A WHIP? $400

$500   WHAT ARE ASSAULT RIFLES? $500

238

JEOPARDY!™

LEGENDS OF SPORTS

Clue	Value	Response
THIS FORMER 49ers QB WHO HOLDS MANY SUPER BOWL RECORDS ALMOST PLAYED COLLEGE BASKETBALL INSTEAD OF FOOTBALL	$100	WHO IS
A BRANTFORD, ONTARIO NATIVE, THIS "GREAT ONE" REWROTE THE NHL RECORD BOOKS	$200	WHO IS
SADLY, THIS UNDEFEATED BOXING LEGEND FROM BROCK-TON, MASSACHUSETTS DIED IN A PLANE CRASH IN 1969	$300	WHO IS
THIS 1932 OLYMPIC GOLD MEDAL WINNER IS OFTEN CALLED THE GREATEST FEMALE ATHLETE OF ALL TIME	$400	WHO IS
HIS LIFETIME BATTING AVERAGE WAS .366— NOT .367, NO MATTER WHAT YOU'VE READ	$500	WHO IS

JEOPARDY!

LEGENDS OF SPORTS

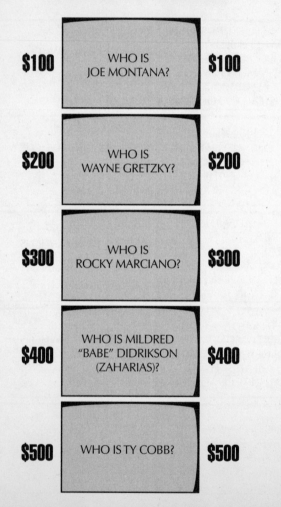

$100 — WHO IS JOE MONTANA? — $100

$200 — WHO IS WAYNE GRETZKY? — $200

$300 — WHO IS ROCKY MARCIANO? — $300

$400 — WHO IS MILDRED "BABE" DIDRIKSON (ZAHARIAS)? — $400

$500 — WHO IS TY COBB? — $500

JEOPARDY!

BRITISH PRIME MINISTERS

HIS LAST TERM AS PRIME MINISTER ENDED IN 1955, THE YEAR HE TURNED 81	**$100**	WHO IS
HE HAD A TOUGH ACT TO FOLLOW: MARGARET THATCHER	**$200**	WHO IS
PM FROM 1937 TO 1940, HE'S LARGELY REMEM-BERED AS A REALLY BAD JUDGE OF CHARACTER	**$300**	WHO IS
THE ELDER WAS PM FROM 1766 TO 1768; THE YOUNGER, FROM 1783 TO 1801 & FROM 1804 TO 1806	**$400**	WHO IS
"MERCIFUL" FIRST NAME OF POSTWAR PM ATTLEE	**$500**	WHAT IS

JEOPARDY!

BRITISH PRIME MINISTERS

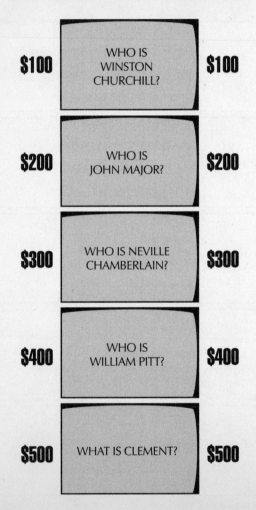

$100   WHO IS WINSTON CHURCHILL?   **$100**

$200   WHO IS JOHN MAJOR?   **$200**

$300   WHO IS NEVILLE CHAMBERLAIN?   **$300**

$400   WHO IS WILLIAM PITT?   **$400**

$500   WHAT IS CLEMENT?   **$500**

JEOPARDY!

I WAS FIRST

Clue	Value	Response
HELLO OUT THERE ... IN 1969 THIS PRESIDENT PLACED THE FIRST TELEPHONE CALL TO THE MOON	$100	WHO IS
IN 1930 ELLEN CHURCH WAS FLYING HIGH AS THE FIRST WOMAN TO SERVE THE AIRLINES IN THIS CAPACITY	$200	WHAT IS
TIRED OF CARRYING 2 PAIRS OF GLASSES AROUND, BENJAMIN FRANKLIN INVENTED THESE	$300	WHAT ARE
MICKEY MOUSE FOUND HIS VOICE IN THIS 1928 CARTOON, THE FIRST TO FEATURE SYNCHRON-IZED SOUND	$400	WHAT IS
A MEMBER OF CONGRESS FROM 1940 TO 1973, THIS DOWN EASTER WAS THE FIRST WOMAN TO SERVE IN THE HOUSE & SENATE	$500	WHO IS

JEOPARDY!

I WAS FIRST

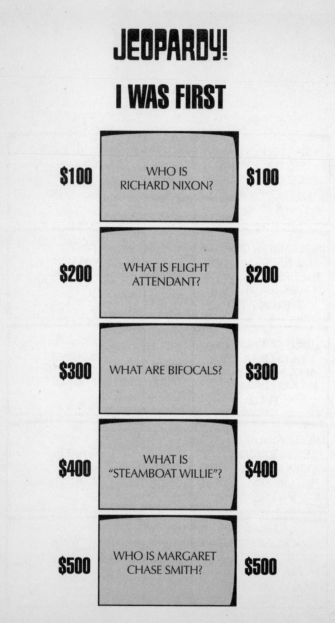

$100   WHO IS RICHARD NIXON? $100

$200   WHAT IS FLIGHT ATTENDANT? $200

$300   WHAT ARE BIFOCALS? $300

$400   WHAT IS "STEAMBOAT WILLIE"? $400

$500   WHO IS MARGARET CHASE SMITH? $500

JEOPARDY!

"SO" WHAT?

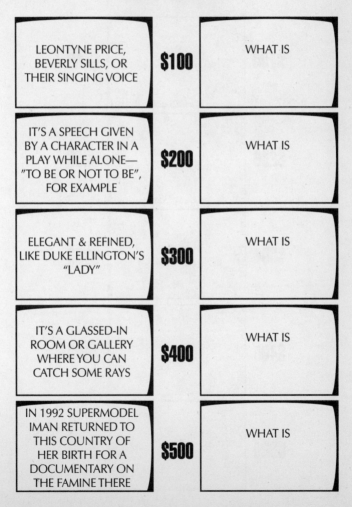

LEONTYNE PRICE, BEVERLY SILLS, OR THEIR SINGING VOICE	$100	WHAT IS
IT'S A SPEECH GIVEN BY A CHARACTER IN A PLAY WHILE ALONE—"TO BE OR NOT TO BE", FOR EXAMPLE	$200	WHAT IS
ELEGANT & REFINED, LIKE DUKE ELLINGTON'S "LADY"	$300	WHAT IS
IT'S A GLASSED-IN ROOM OR GALLERY WHERE YOU CAN CATCH SOME RAYS	$400	WHAT IS
IN 1992 SUPERMODEL IMAN RETURNED TO THIS COUNTRY OF HER BIRTH FOR A DOCUMENTARY ON THE FAMINE THERE	$500	WHAT IS

JEOPARDY!

"SO" WHAT?

$100	WHAT IS SOPRANO?	$100
$200	WHAT IS A SOLILOQUY?	$200
$300	WHAT IS SOPHISTICATED?	$300
$400	WHAT IS A SOLARIUM?	$400
$500	WHAT IS SOMALIA?	$500

DOUBLE JEOPARDY!

OPERA

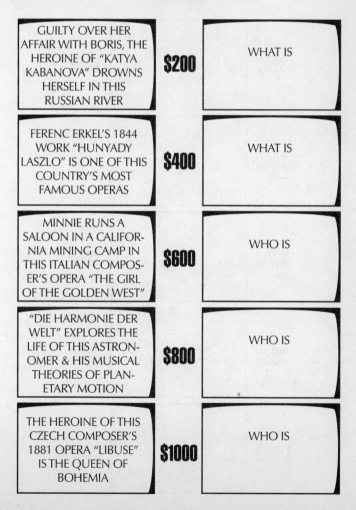

Clue	Value	Response
GUILTY OVER HER AFFAIR WITH BORIS, THE HEROINE OF "KATYA KABANOVA" DROWNS HERSELF IN THIS RUSSIAN RIVER	$200	WHAT IS
FERENC ERKEL'S 1844 WORK "HUNYADY LASZLO" IS ONE OF THIS COUNTRY'S MOST FAMOUS OPERAS	$400	WHAT IS
MINNIE RUNS A SALOON IN A CALIFORNIA MINING CAMP IN THIS ITALIAN COMPOSER'S OPERA "THE GIRL OF THE GOLDEN WEST"	$600	WHO IS
"DIE HARMONIE DER WELT" EXPLORES THE LIFE OF THIS ASTRONOMER & HIS MUSICAL THEORIES OF PLANETARY MOTION	$800	WHO IS
THE HEROINE OF THIS CZECH COMPOSER'S 1881 OPERA "LIBUSE" IS THE QUEEN OF BOHEMIA	$1000	WHO IS

DOUBLE JEOPARDY!

OPERA

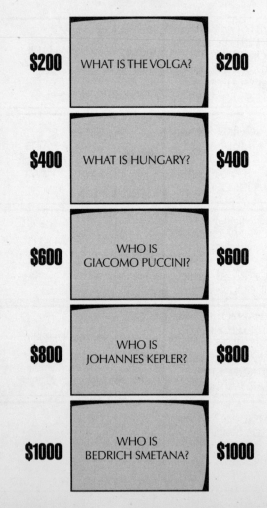

$200	WHAT IS THE VOLGA? **$200**
$400	WHAT IS HUNGARY? **$400**
$600	WHO IS GIACOMO PUCCINI? **$600**
$800	WHO IS JOHANNES KEPLER? **$800**
$1000	WHO IS BEDRICH SMETANA? **$1000**

DOUBLE JEOPARDY!

1980s FADS

TORN SWEATSHIRTS & LEGWARMERS WERE ALL THE RAGE AFTER THIS 1983 JENNIFER BEALS MOVIE	**$200**	WHAT IS
SENSITIVE MEN OF THE '70s WERE OUT; "REAL MEN" DIDN'T EAT THIS	**$400**	WHAT IS
ANDROGYNY WAS EXEMPLIFIED BY EURYTHMICS' ANNIE LENNOX, & BY THIS LEAD SINGER OF THE CULTURE CLUB	**$600**	WHO IS
BASED ON XAVIER ROBERTS' SCULPTURES, THESE DOLLS WERE A POPULAR ITEM FOR ADOPTION IN 1983	**$800**	WHAT ARE
GREED WAS GOOD: TRUMP TAUGHT "THE ART OF THE DEAL", & SHE SAID, "ONLY THE LITTLE PEOPLE PAY TAXES"	**$1000**	WHO IS

DOUBLE JEOPARDY!

1980s FADS

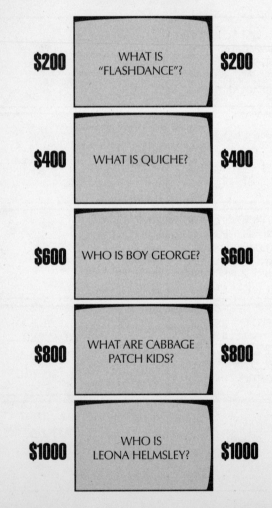

$200	WHAT IS "FLASHDANCE"?	$200
$400	WHAT IS QUICHE?	$400
$600	WHO IS BOY GEORGE?	$600
$800	WHAT ARE CABBAGE PATCH KIDS?	$800
$1000	WHO IS LEONA HELMSLEY?	$1000

DOUBLE JEOPARDY!

INVENTORS

THIS PHONOGRAPH INVENTOR'S SON CHARLES SERVED AS GOVERNOR OF NEW JERSEY FROM 1941 TO 1944	**$200**	WHO IS
AROUND 1045 PI SHENG CAME UP WITH THIS MOVABLE INVENTION, LATER USED BY GUTENBERG	**$400**	WHAT IS
IN 1857 THIS TELEGRAPH INVENTOR SERVED AS THE ELECTRICIAN ON CYRUS FIELD'S FIRST TRANSATLANTIC CABLE ATTEMPT	**$600**	WHO IS
IN THE 1850s HE PATENTED THE FOOT TREADLE FOR HIS SEWING MACHINE	**$800**	WHO IS
IN 1854 HORACE SMITH & THIS PARTNER PATENTED THE REPEATING RIFLE & REVOLVER	**$1000**	WHO IS

DOUBLE JEOPARDY!

INVENTORS

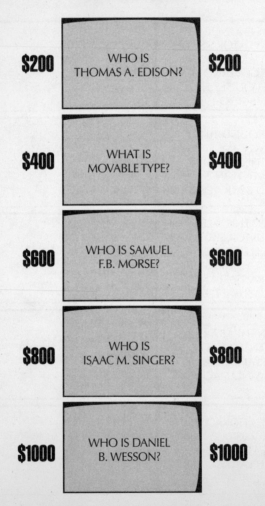

$200   WHO IS THOMAS A. EDISON? $200

$400   WHAT IS MOVABLE TYPE? $400

$600   WHO IS SAMUEL F.B. MORSE? $600

$800   WHO IS ISAAC M. SINGER? $800

$1000   WHO IS DANIEL B. WESSON? $1000

DOUBLE JEOPARDY!

A CINEMATIC TRIP TO VEGAS

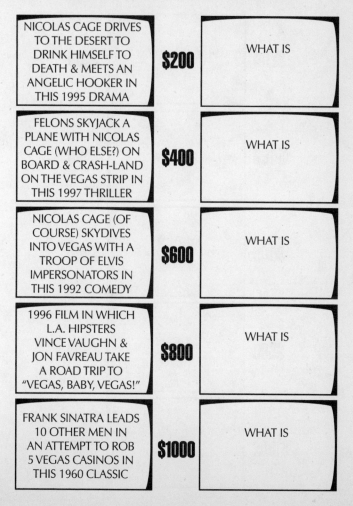

NICOLAS CAGE DRIVES TO THE DESERT TO DRINK HIMSELF TO DEATH & MEETS AN ANGELIC HOOKER IN THIS 1995 DRAMA	**$200**	WHAT IS
FELONS SKYJACK A PLANE WITH NICOLAS CAGE (WHO ELSE?) ON BOARD & CRASH-LAND ON THE VEGAS STRIP IN THIS 1997 THRILLER	**$400**	WHAT IS
NICOLAS CAGE (OF COURSE) SKYDIVES INTO VEGAS WITH A TROOP OF ELVIS IMPERSONATORS IN THIS 1992 COMEDY	**$600**	WHAT IS
1996 FILM IN WHICH L.A. HIPSTERS VINCE VAUGHN & JON FAVREAU TAKE A ROAD TRIP TO "VEGAS, BABY, VEGAS!"	**$800**	WHAT IS
FRANK SINATRA LEADS 10 OTHER MEN IN AN ATTEMPT TO ROB 5 VEGAS CASINOS IN THIS 1960 CLASSIC	**$1000**	WHAT IS

DOUBLE JEOPARDY!

A CINEMATIC TRIP TO VEGAS

$200   WHAT IS "LEAVING LAS VEGAS"? $200

$400   WHAT IS "CON AIR"? $400

$600   WHAT IS "HONEYMOON IN VEGAS"? $600

$800   WHAT IS "SWINGERS"? $800

$1000   WHAT IS "OCEAN'S ELEVEN"? $1000

DOUBLE JEOPARDY!

ANCIENT HISTORY

THIS COUNTRY'S SHANG DYNASTY AROSE IN THE 1700s B.C. ALONG THE YELLOW RIVER	**$200**	WHAT IS
IN 439 A.D. THIS NORTH AFRICAN CITY-STATE WAS CONQUERED BY THE VANDALS UNDER GENSERIC	**$400**	WHAT IS
IN 303 A.D. DIOCLETIAN FORBADE CHRISTIAN WORSHIP; THIS MAN, HIS "GREAT" SUCCESSOR, REVOKED THE EDICT 10 YEARS LATER	**$600**	WHO IS
SCULPTURE BY SCOPAS DECORATED THIS TOMB AT HALICARNASSUS, ONE OF THE 7 ANCIENT WONDERS	**$800**	WHAT IS
WHEN HE DIED AROUND 347 B.C., HIS NEPHEW SPEUSIPPUS TOOK OVER LEADERSHIP OF THE ACADEMY	**$1000**	WHO IS

DOUBLE JEOPARDY!

ANCIENT HISTORY

$200	WHAT IS CHINA?	$200
$400	WHAT IS CARTHAGE?	$400
$600	WHO IS CONSTANTINE (I OR THE GREAT)?	$600
$800	WHAT IS THE MAUSOLEUM?	$800
$1000	WHO IS PLATO?	$1000

DOUBLE JEOPARDY!

3-LETTER WORDS

IT'S ONE LAYER OF TOILET PAPER OR WOOD	**$200**	WHAT IS
A YOUNG FISH, A WAY TO COOK IT, OR A "SMALL" (UNIMPORTANT) PERSON	**$400**	WHAT IS
AN EYE IRRITATION, OR A PIGPEN	**$600**	WHAT IS
A LARGE COFFEE CONTAINER, OR A LARGE VASE TO STASH ONE'S ASHES	**$800**	WHAT IS
IT EQUALS 1/1000th OF AN INCH	**$1000**	WHAT IS

DOUBLE JEOPARDY!

3-LETTER WORDS

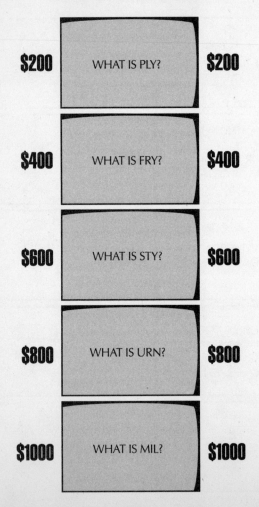

$200   WHAT IS PLY? $200

$400   WHAT IS FRY? $400

$600   WHAT IS STY? $600

$800   WHAT IS URN? $800

$1000   WHAT IS MIL? $1000

FINAL JEOPARDY!
FAMOUS WOMEN

DURING WWI THIS
AMERICAN SHOWED OFF
HER TALENTS IN A PLAY
CALLED "THE WESTERN GIRL"

WHO IS

FINAL JEOPARDY!

FAMOUS WOMEN

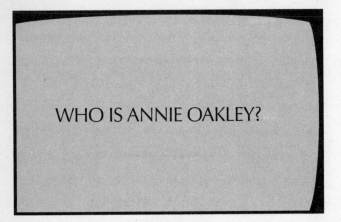

WHO IS ANNIE OAKLEY?

JEOPARDY!™

HISTORY

Clue	Value	Response
1903's TREATY OF PETROPOLIS "ERASED" A SOUTH AMERICAN DISPUTE OVER AN AREA RICH IN THIS PLANT RESOURCE	$100	WHAT IS
IN 1931 THE INVADING JAPANESE MADE THIS CHINESE AREA A PUPPET STATE CALLED MANCHUKUO	$200	WHAT IS
THE LIMITED IRISH AUTONOMY PROPOSED BY ISAAC BUTT AROUND 1870 WAS CALLED THIS TYPE OF "RULE"	$300	WHAT IS
BRUGGE IN FLEMISH, THIS BELGIAN CITY'S TRADE DECLINED WITH THE SILTING OF THE ZWYN RIVER IN THE 1400s	$400	WHAT IS
IN 897 POPE STEPHEN VI HAD HIS PREDECESSOR FORMOSUS EXHUMED, PUT ON TRIAL & THROWN INTO THIS RIVER	$500	WHAT IS

JEOPARDY!™

HISTORY

$100	WHAT IS RUBBER?	**$100**
$200	WHAT IS MANCHURIA?	**$200**
$300	WHAT IS HOME RULE?	**$300**
$400	WHAT IS BRUGES?	**$400**
$500	WHAT IS THE TIBER?	**$500**

JEOPARDY!

ANIMAL BEHAVIOR

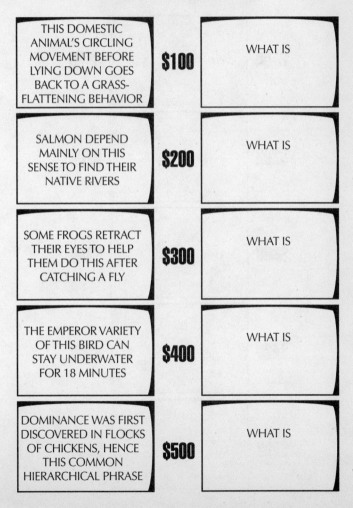

THIS DOMESTIC ANIMAL'S CIRCLING MOVEMENT BEFORE LYING DOWN GOES BACK TO A GRASS-FLATTENING BEHAVIOR	**$100**	WHAT IS
SALMON DEPEND MAINLY ON THIS SENSE TO FIND THEIR NATIVE RIVERS	**$200**	WHAT IS
SOME FROGS RETRACT THEIR EYES TO HELP THEM DO THIS AFTER CATCHING A FLY	**$300**	WHAT IS
THE EMPEROR VARIETY OF THIS BIRD CAN STAY UNDERWATER FOR 18 MINUTES	**$400**	WHAT IS
DOMINANCE WAS FIRST DISCOVERED IN FLOCKS OF CHICKENS, HENCE THIS COMMON HIERARCHICAL PHRASE	**$500**	WHAT IS

JEOPARDY!

ANIMAL BEHAVIOR

$100 — WHAT IS THE DOG? — $100

$200 — WHAT IS SMELL? — $200

$300 — WHAT IS SWALLOW? — $300

$400 — WHAT IS THE PENGUIN? — $400

$500 — WHAT IS PECK(ING) ORDER? — $500

JEOPARDY!

FILM FOLK

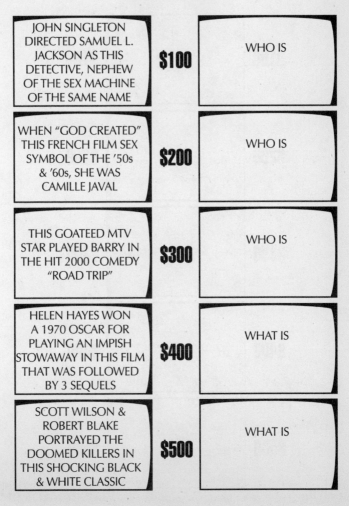

JOHN SINGLETON DIRECTED SAMUEL L. JACKSON AS THIS DETECTIVE, NEPHEW OF THE SEX MACHINE OF THE SAME NAME	$100	WHO IS
WHEN "GOD CREATED" THIS FRENCH FILM SEX SYMBOL OF THE '50s & '60s, SHE WAS CAMILLE JAVAL	$200	WHO IS
THIS GOATEED MTV STAR PLAYED BARRY IN THE HIT 2000 COMEDY "ROAD TRIP"	$300	WHO IS
HELEN HAYES WON A 1970 OSCAR FOR PLAYING AN IMPISH STOWAWAY IN THIS FILM THAT WAS FOLLOWED BY 3 SEQUELS	$400	WHAT IS
SCOTT WILSON & ROBERT BLAKE PORTRAYED THE DOOMED KILLERS IN THIS SHOCKING BLACK & WHITE CLASSIC	$500	WHAT IS

JEOPARDY!

FILM FOLK

$100 — WHO IS JOHN SHAFT? — $100

$200 — WHO IS BRIGITTE BARDOT? — $200

$300 — WHO IS TOM GREEN? — $300

$400 — WHAT IS "AIRPORT"? — $400

$500 — WHAT IS "IN COLD BLOOD"? — $500

JEOPARDY!

LITERARY SAN FRANCISCO

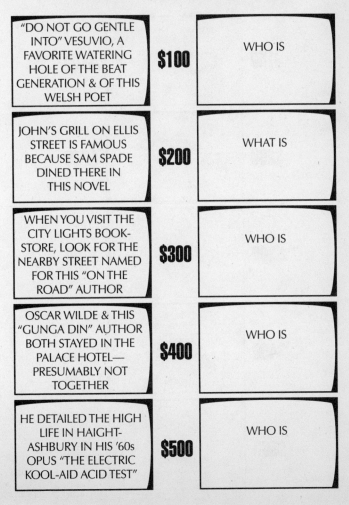

Clue	Value	Response
"DO NOT GO GENTLE INTO" VESUVIO, A FAVORITE WATERING HOLE OF THE BEAT GENERATION & OF THIS WELSH POET	$100	WHO IS
JOHN'S GRILL ON ELLIS STREET IS FAMOUS BECAUSE SAM SPADE DINED THERE IN THIS NOVEL	$200	WHAT IS
WHEN YOU VISIT THE CITY LIGHTS BOOK-STORE, LOOK FOR THE NEARBY STREET NAMED FOR THIS "ON THE ROAD" AUTHOR	$300	WHO IS
OSCAR WILDE & THIS "GUNGA DIN" AUTHOR BOTH STAYED IN THE PALACE HOTEL— PRESUMABLY NOT TOGETHER	$400	WHO IS
HE DETAILED THE HIGH LIFE IN HAIGHT-ASHBURY IN HIS '60s OPUS "THE ELECTRIC KOOL-AID ACID TEST"	$500	WHO IS

JEOPARDY!

LITERARY SAN FRANCISCO

$100 · WHO IS DYLAN THOMAS? · $100

$200 · WHAT IS "THE MALTESE FALCON"? · $200

$300 · WHO IS JACK KEROUAC? · $300

$400 · WHO IS RUDYARD KIPLING? · $400

$500 · WHO IS TOM WOLFE? · $500

JEOPARDY!

HOLIDAYS & OBSERVANCES

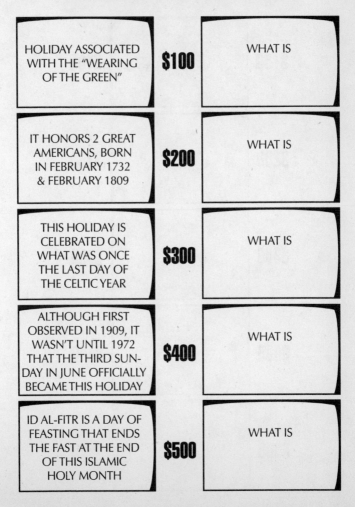

HOLIDAY ASSOCIATED WITH THE "WEARING OF THE GREEN"	$100	WHAT IS
IT HONORS 2 GREAT AMERICANS, BORN IN FEBRUARY 1732 & FEBRUARY 1809	$200	WHAT IS
THIS HOLIDAY IS CELEBRATED ON WHAT WAS ONCE THE LAST DAY OF THE CELTIC YEAR	$300	WHAT IS
ALTHOUGH FIRST OBSERVED IN 1909, IT WASN'T UNTIL 1972 THAT THE THIRD SUNDAY IN JUNE OFFICIALLY BECAME THIS HOLIDAY	$400	WHAT IS
ID AL-FITR IS A DAY OF FEASTING THAT ENDS THE FAST AT THE END OF THIS ISLAMIC HOLY MONTH	$500	WHAT IS

JEOPARDY!™

HOLIDAYS & OBSERVANCES

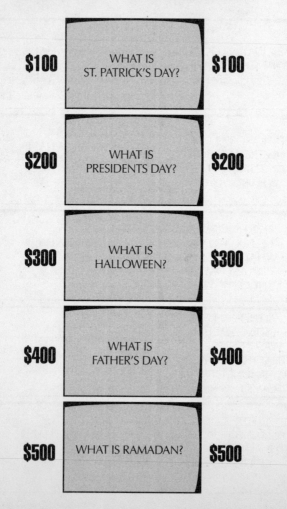

$100   WHAT IS ST. PATRICK'S DAY? $100

$200   WHAT IS PRESIDENTS DAY? $200

$300   WHAT IS HALLOWEEN? $300

$400   WHAT IS FATHER'S DAY? $400

$500   WHAT IS RAMADAN? $500

JEOPARDY!

"WHOLE"SOME

IF FREDDY, WILBUR OR BABE INDULGED HIMSELF COMPLETELY, HE'D "GO" THIS	$100	WHAT IS
A COMPLETELY FICTITIOUS TALE IS "MADE OUT OF" THIS	$200	WHAT IS
IN A JOKING W.C. FIELDS EPITAPH, THESE 3 WORDS PRECEDE "I'D RATHER BE IN PHILADELPHIA"	$300	WHAT ARE
SHEBEEN, A WORD FOR AN IRISH TAVERN, MAY BE THE ORIGIN OF THIS EXPRESSION	$400	WHAT IS
COMPLETES THE FAMOUS ALKA-SELTZER AD LINE, "I CAN'T BELIEVE . . ."	$500	WHAT IS

271

JEOPARDY!

"WHOLE"SOME

$100   WHAT IS WHOLE HOG? $100

$200   WHAT IS WHOLE CLOTH? $200

$300   WHAT ARE "ON THE WHOLE"? $300

$400   WHAT IS THE WHOLE SHEBANG? $400

$500   WHAT IS "I ATE THE WHOLE THING"? $500

DOUBLE JEOPARDY!

THE MIDWEST

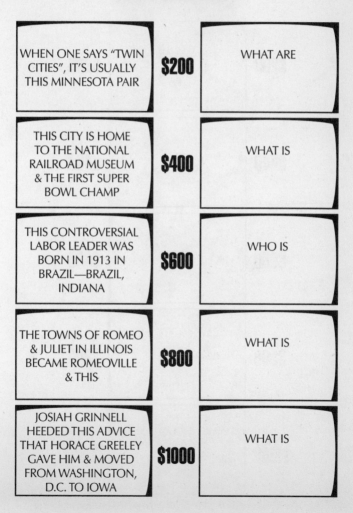

Clue	Value	Response
WHEN ONE SAYS "TWIN CITIES", IT'S USUALLY THIS MINNESOTA PAIR	$200	WHAT ARE
THIS CITY IS HOME TO THE NATIONAL RAILROAD MUSEUM & THE FIRST SUPER BOWL CHAMP	$400	WHAT IS
THIS CONTROVERSIAL LABOR LEADER WAS BORN IN 1913 IN BRAZIL—BRAZIL, INDIANA	$600	WHO IS
THE TOWNS OF ROMEO & JULIET IN ILLINOIS BECAME ROMEOVILLE & THIS	$800	WHAT IS
JOSIAH GRINNELL HEEDED THIS ADVICE THAT HORACE GREELEY GAVE HIM & MOVED FROM WASHINGTON, D.C. TO IOWA	$1000	WHAT IS

DOUBLE JEOPARDY!

THE MIDWEST

$200 — WHAT ARE MINNEAPOLIS & ST. PAUL? — $200

$400 — WHAT IS GREEN BAY (WISCONSIN)? — $400

$600 — WHO IS JIMMY HOFFA? — $600

$800 — WHAT IS JOLIET? — $800

$1000 — WHAT IS "GO WEST YOUNG MAN (AND GROW UP WITH THE COUNTRY)"? — $1000

DOUBLE JEOPARDY!

THE NUDE IN ART

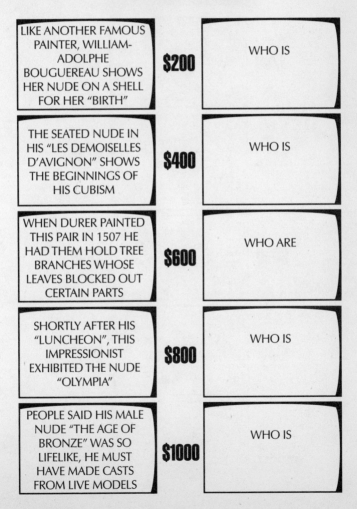

LIKE ANOTHER FAMOUS PAINTER, WILLIAM-ADOLPHE BOUGUEREAU SHOWS HER NUDE ON A SHELL FOR HER "BIRTH"	$200	WHO IS
THE SEATED NUDE IN HIS "LES DEMOISELLES D'AVIGNON" SHOWS THE BEGINNINGS OF HIS CUBISM	$400	WHO IS
WHEN DURER PAINTED THIS PAIR IN 1507 HE HAD THEM HOLD TREE BRANCHES WHOSE LEAVES BLOCKED OUT CERTAIN PARTS	$600	WHO ARE
SHORTLY AFTER HIS "LUNCHEON", THIS IMPRESSIONIST EXHIBITED THE NUDE "OLYMPIA"	$800	WHO IS
PEOPLE SAID HIS MALE NUDE "THE AGE OF BRONZE" WAS SO LIFELIKE, HE MUST HAVE MADE CASTS FROM LIVE MODELS	$1000	WHO IS

DOUBLE JEOPARDY!

THE NUDE IN ART

$200   WHO IS VENUS? $200

$400   WHO IS PABLO PICASSO? $400

$600   WHO ARE ADAM & EVE? $600

$800   WHO IS EDOUARD MANET? $800

$1000   WHO IS AUGUSTE RODIN? $1000

DOUBLE JEOPARDY!

THE SPORTING LIFE

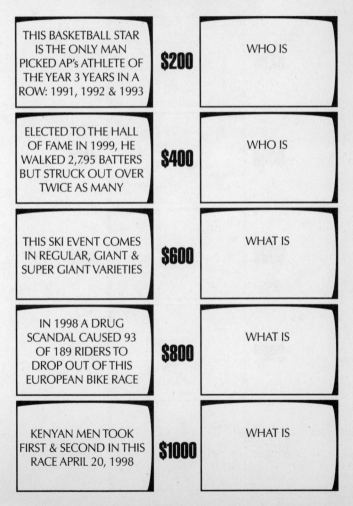

THIS BASKETBALL STAR IS THE ONLY MAN PICKED AP's ATHLETE OF THE YEAR 3 YEARS IN A ROW: 1991, 1992 & 1993	**$200**	WHO IS
ELECTED TO THE HALL OF FAME IN 1999, HE WALKED 2,795 BATTERS BUT STRUCK OUT OVER TWICE AS MANY	**$400**	WHO IS
THIS SKI EVENT COMES IN REGULAR, GIANT & SUPER GIANT VARIETIES	**$600**	WHAT IS
IN 1998 A DRUG SCANDAL CAUSED 93 OF 189 RIDERS TO DROP OUT OF THIS EUROPEAN BIKE RACE	**$800**	WHAT IS
KENYAN MEN TOOK FIRST & SECOND IN THIS RACE APRIL 20, 1998	**$1000**	WHAT IS

DOUBLE JEOPARDY!

THE SPORTING LIFE

$200 WHO IS MICHAEL JORDAN? **$200**

$400 WHO IS NOLAN RYAN? **$400**

$600 WHAT IS THE SLALOM? **$600**

$800 WHAT IS THE TOUR DE FRANCE? **$800**

$1000 WHAT IS THE BOSTON MARATHON? **$1000**

DOUBLE JEOPARDY!

THEORIES

THE THEORY THAT LED TO REAGANOMICS GOT THIS NAME BY OPPOSING THE TRADITIONAL FOCUS ON DEMAND	**$200**	WHAT IS
DARWIN CALLED HIS BOOK "ON THE ORIGIN OF SPECIES BY MEANS OF NATURAL" THIS	**$400**	WHAT IS
A 1944 BOOK LAUNCHED THIS FIELD THAT CAN DISSECT ACTIVITIES LIKE POKER & CHECKERS	**$600**	WHAT IS
OPPOSED TO THE BIG BANG THEORY, SIR FRED HOYLE DEVELOPED THIS THEORY OF A CONSISTENT UNIVERSE	**$800**	WHAT IS
THORSTEIN VEBLEN COINED "CONSPICUOUS CONSUMPTION" IN "THE THEORY OF" THIS "CLASS"	**$1000**	WHAT IS

DOUBLE JEOPARDY!

THEORIES

$200 WHAT IS SUPPLY-SIDE ECONOMICS? **$200**

$400 WHAT IS SELECTION? **$400**

$600 WHAT IS GAME THEORY? **$600**

$800 WHAT IS THE STEADY-STATE THEORY? **$800**

$1000 WHAT IS THE LEISURE CLASS? **$1000**

DOUBLE JEOPARDY!

A BIT WORDY

WHAT THE OLD NORSE KNEW AS THORSDAGR, WE CALL THIS TODAY	**$200**	WHAT IS
OF A PERSON, PLACE OR THING, IT'S WHAT THE ROSETTA STONE WAS NAMED FOR	**$400**	WHAT IS
FROM THE GREEK FOR A "RACE DISCOURSE", IT'S THE HISTORY OF A FAMILY	**$600**	WHAT IS
THE WORDS JOURNEY, JOURNAL & DIURNAL ARE ALL BASED ON THIS UNIT OF TIME	**$800**	WHAT IS
ALONE IT MEANS "SILENCE"; ADD "BLE" & IT MEANS TO TALK INDISTINCTLY	**$1000**	WHAT IS

DOUBLE JEOPARDY!

A BIT WORDY

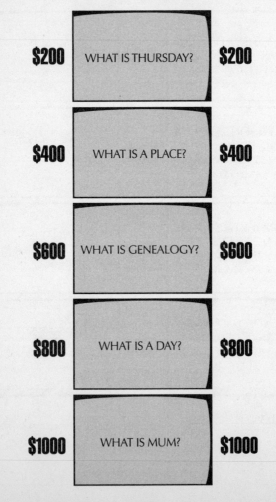

$200   WHAT IS THURSDAY? $200

$400   WHAT IS A PLACE? $400

$600   WHAT IS GENEALOGY? $600

$800   WHAT IS A DAY? $800

$1000   WHAT IS MUM? $1000

DOUBLE JEOPARDY!

HISS-STORY

TRADITION SAYS THAT IN AUGUST 30 B.C. SHE COMMITTED SUICIDE WITH THE BITE OF AN ASP, A SYMBOL OF DIVINE ROYALTY	**$200**	WHO IS
IN GENESIS 3:13 EVE SAID, THIS CREATURE "BEGUILED ME, AND I DID EAT"	**$400**	WHAT IS
PATRIOTIC FLAGS OF THE AMERICAN REVOLUTION DEPICTED A COILED TIMBER RATTLESNAKE & THIS MOTTO	**$600**	WHAT IS
REPTILIAN NICKNAME USED FOR UNION DEM-OCRATS WHO OPPOSED LINCOLN'S EFFORTS TO FREE THE SLAVES DURING THE CIVIL WAR	**$800**	WHAT ARE
THIS ANCIENT WINGED STAFF FEATURING 2 INTERTWINED SNAKES IS NOW THE SYMBOL OF THE U.S. ARMY MEDICAL CORPS	**$1000**	WHAT IS

DOUBLE JEOPARDY!

HISS-STORY

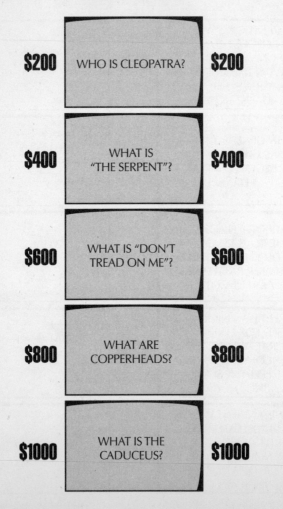

$200 WHO IS CLEOPATRA? **$200**

$400 WHAT IS "THE SERPENT"? **$400**

$600 WHAT IS "DON'T TREAD ON ME"? **$600**

$800 WHAT ARE COPPERHEADS? **$800**

$1000 WHAT IS THE CADUCEUS? **$1000**

FINAL JEOPARDY!

BUSINESS & INDUSTRY

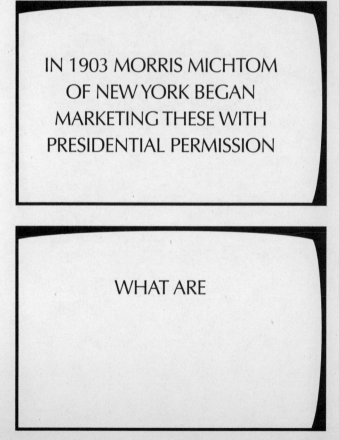

IN 1903 MORRIS MICHTOM
OF NEW YORK BEGAN
MARKETING THESE WITH
PRESIDENTIAL PERMISSION

WHAT ARE

FINAL JEOPARDY!

BUSINESS & INDUSTRY

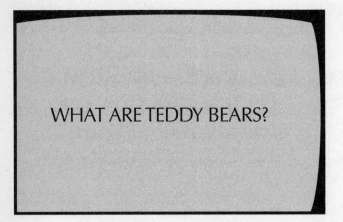

WHAT ARE TEDDY BEARS?

JEOPARDY!

TRAVEL & TOURISM

THIS SITE NEAR SALISBURY, ENGLAND HAS HUGE BOULDERS THAT MAY HAVE COME FROM SOUTHERN WALES	**$100**	WHAT IS
DOW'S LAKE IS PROBABLY THE BEST PLACE TO VIEW THE TULIPS DURING THIS CANADIAN CAPITAL'S MAY TULIP FESTIVAL	**$200**	WHAT IS
THIS COUNTRY'S TIKAL RUINS WERE ONCE A CEREMONIAL CENTER & THE LARGEST CITY OF THE MAYAN EMPIRE	**$300**	WHAT IS
THIS OLYMPIC CITY'S FAMOUS SITES INCLUDE A HARBOUR BRIDGE & AN OPERA HOUSE	**$400**	WHAT IS
THIS STONE PILLAR "OF LUXOR" STANDS 75 FEET HIGH IN THE PLACE DE LA CONCORDE IN PARIS	**$500**	WHAT IS

JEOPARDY!™

TRAVEL & TOURISM

$100 WHAT IS STONEHENGE? $100

$200 WHAT IS OTTAWA? $200

$300 WHAT IS GUATEMALA? $300

$400 WHAT IS SYDNEY? $400

$500 WHAT IS THE OBELISK OF LUXOR? $500

JEOPARDY!

SECRETARIES OF COMMERCE

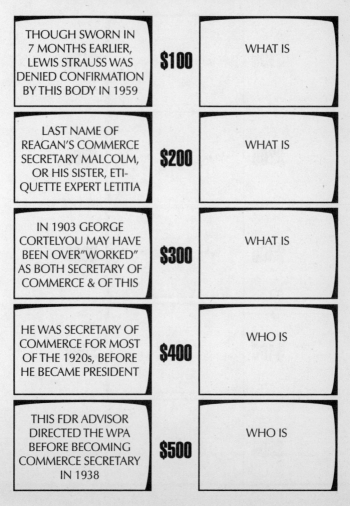

THOUGH SWORN IN 7 MONTHS EARLIER, LEWIS STRAUSS WAS DENIED CONFIRMATION BY THIS BODY IN 1959	**$100**	WHAT IS
LAST NAME OF REAGAN'S COMMERCE SECRETARY MALCOLM, OR HIS SISTER, ETIQUETTE EXPERT LETITIA	**$200**	WHAT IS
IN 1903 GEORGE CORTELYOU MAY HAVE BEEN OVER"WORKED" AS BOTH SECRETARY OF COMMERCE & OF THIS	**$300**	WHAT IS
HE WAS SECRETARY OF COMMERCE FOR MOST OF THE 1920s, BEFORE HE BECAME PRESIDENT	**$400**	WHO IS
THIS FDR ADVISOR DIRECTED THE WPA BEFORE BECOMING COMMERCE SECRETARY IN 1938	**$500**	WHO IS

JEOPARDY!

SECRETARIES OF COMMERCE

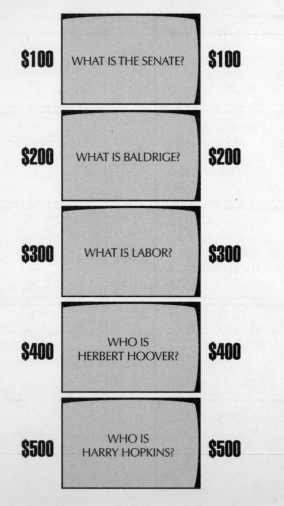

$100 — WHAT IS THE SENATE? — **$100**

$200 — WHAT IS BALDRIGE? — **$200**

$300 — WHAT IS LABOR? — **$300**

$400 — WHO IS HERBERT HOOVER? — **$400**

$500 — WHO IS HARRY HOPKINS? — **$500**

JEOPARDY!

CIVIL WAR SLANG

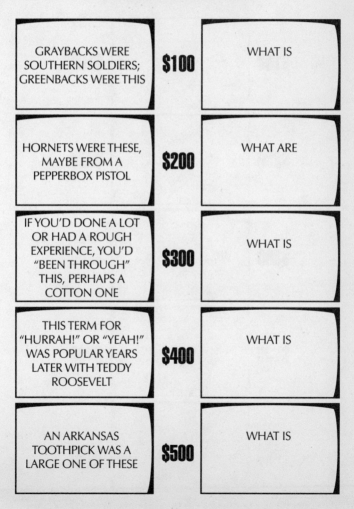

Clue	Value	Response
GRAYBACKS WERE SOUTHERN SOLDIERS; GREENBACKS WERE THIS	**$100**	WHAT IS
HORNETS WERE THESE, MAYBE FROM A PEPPERBOX PISTOL	**$200**	WHAT ARE
IF YOU'D DONE A LOT OR HAD A ROUGH EXPERIENCE, YOU'D "BEEN THROUGH" THIS, PERHAPS A COTTON ONE	**$300**	WHAT IS
THIS TERM FOR "HURRAH!" OR "YEAH!" WAS POPULAR YEARS LATER WITH TEDDY ROOSEVELT	**$400**	WHAT IS
AN ARKANSAS TOOTHPICK WAS A LARGE ONE OF THESE	**$500**	WHAT IS

JEOPARDY!

CIVIL WAR SLANG

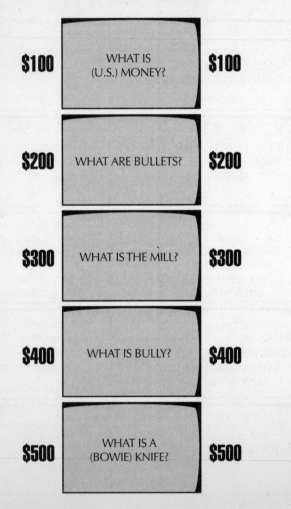

$100	WHAT IS (U.S.) MONEY?
$200	WHAT ARE BULLETS?
$300	WHAT IS THE MILL?
$400	WHAT IS BULLY?
$500	WHAT IS A (BOWIE) KNIFE?

JEOPARDY!

SPOUSE IN COMMON

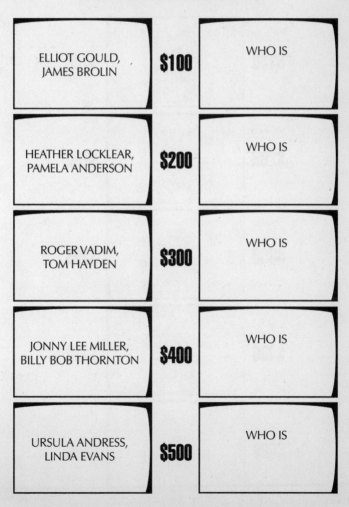

ELLIOT GOULD, JAMES BROLIN	$100	WHO IS
HEATHER LOCKLEAR, PAMELA ANDERSON	$200	WHO IS
ROGER VADIM, TOM HAYDEN	$300	WHO IS
JONNY LEE MILLER, BILLY BOB THORNTON	$400	WHO IS
URSULA ANDRESS, LINDA EVANS	$500	WHO IS

JEOPARDY!

SPOUSE IN COMMON

$100   WHO IS BARBRA STREISAND? $100

$200   WHO IS TOMMY LEE? $200

$300   WHO IS JANE FONDA? $300

$400   WHO IS ANGELINA JOLIE? $400

$500   WHO IS JOHN DEREK? $500

JEOPARDY!

POETS & POETRY

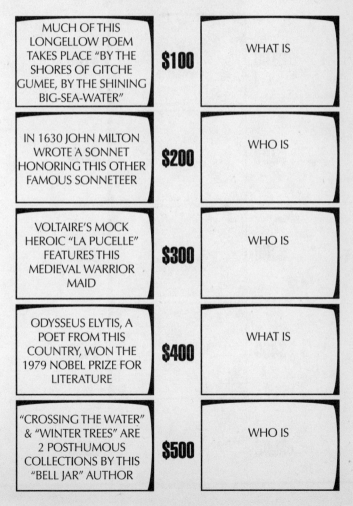

MUCH OF THIS LONGFELLOW POEM TAKES PLACE "BY THE SHORES OF GITCHE GUMEE, BY THE SHINING BIG-SEA-WATER"	**$100**	WHAT IS
IN 1630 JOHN MILTON WROTE A SONNET HONORING THIS OTHER FAMOUS SONNETEER	**$200**	WHO IS
VOLTAIRE'S MOCK HEROIC "LA PUCELLE" FEATURES THIS MEDIEVAL WARRIOR MAID	**$300**	WHO IS
ODYSSEUS ELYTIS, A POET FROM THIS COUNTRY, WON THE 1979 NOBEL PRIZE FOR LITERATURE	**$400**	WHAT IS
"CROSSING THE WATER" & "WINTER TREES" ARE 2 POSTHUMOUS COLLECTIONS BY THIS "BELL JAR" AUTHOR	**$500**	WHO IS

JEOPARDY!

POETS & POETRY

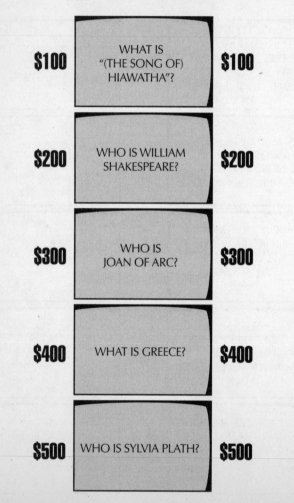

$100	WHAT IS "(THE SONG OF) HIAWATHA"?	**$100**
$200	WHO IS WILLIAM SHAKESPEARE?	**$200**
$300	WHO IS JOAN OF ARC?	**$300**
$400	WHAT IS GREECE?	**$400**
$500	WHO IS SYLVIA PLATH?	**$500**

JEOPARDY!

THEY MEANT BUSINESS

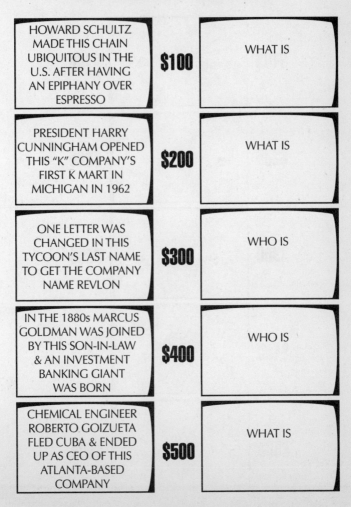

HOWARD SCHULTZ MADE THIS CHAIN UBIQUITOUS IN THE U.S. AFTER HAVING AN EPIPHANY OVER ESPRESSO	**$100**	WHAT IS
PRESIDENT HARRY CUNNINGHAM OPENED THIS "K" COMPANY'S FIRST K MART IN MICHIGAN IN 1962	**$200**	WHAT IS
ONE LETTER WAS CHANGED IN THIS TYCOON'S LAST NAME TO GET THE COMPANY NAME REVLON	**$300**	WHO IS
IN THE 1880s MARCUS GOLDMAN WAS JOINED BY THIS SON-IN-LAW & AN INVESTMENT BANKING GIANT WAS BORN	**$400**	WHO IS
CHEMICAL ENGINEER ROBERTO GOIZUETA FLED CUBA & ENDED UP AS CEO OF THIS ATLANTA-BASED COMPANY	**$500**	WHAT IS

JEOPARDY!

THEY MEANT BUSINESS

$100 WHAT IS STARBUCKS? $100

$200 WHAT IS S.S. KRESGE? $200

$300 WHO IS CHARLES REVSON? $300

$400 WHO IS SAMUEL SACHS? $400

$500 WHAT IS COCA-COLA? $500

DOUBLE JEOPARDY!

SCIENCE

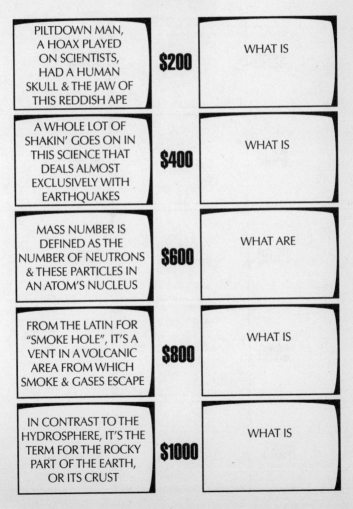

PILTDOWN MAN, A HOAX PLAYED ON SCIENTISTS, HAD A HUMAN SKULL & THE JAW OF THIS REDDISH APE	**$200**	WHAT IS
A WHOLE LOT OF SHAKIN' GOES ON IN THIS SCIENCE THAT DEALS ALMOST EXCLUSIVELY WITH EARTHQUAKES	**$400**	WHAT IS
MASS NUMBER IS DEFINED AS THE NUMBER OF NEUTRONS & THESE PARTICLES IN AN ATOM'S NUCLEUS	**$600**	WHAT ARE
FROM THE LATIN FOR "SMOKE HOLE", IT'S A VENT IN A VOLCANIC AREA FROM WHICH SMOKE & GASES ESCAPE	**$800**	WHAT IS
IN CONTRAST TO THE HYDROSPHERE, IT'S THE TERM FOR THE ROCKY PART OF THE EARTH, OR ITS CRUST	**$1000**	WHAT IS

DOUBLE JEOPARDY!

SCIENCE

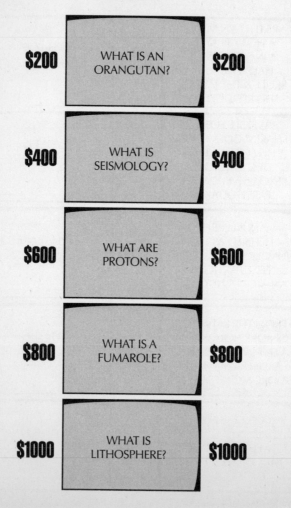

$200 — WHAT IS AN ORANGUTAN? — $200

$400 — WHAT IS SEISMOLOGY? — $400

$600 — WHAT ARE PROTONS? — $600

$800 — WHAT IS A FUMAROLE? — $800

$1000 — WHAT IS LITHOSPHERE? — $1000

DOUBLE JEOPARDY!

JUST DESSERTS

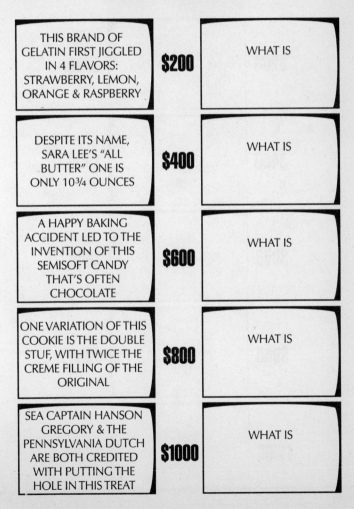

THIS BRAND OF GELATIN FIRST JIGGLED IN 4 FLAVORS: STRAWBERRY, LEMON, ORANGE & RASPBERRY	**$200**	WHAT IS
DESPITE ITS NAME, SARA LEE'S "ALL BUTTER" ONE IS ONLY 10¾ OUNCES	**$400**	WHAT IS
A HAPPY BAKING ACCIDENT LED TO THE INVENTION OF THIS SEMISOFT CANDY THAT'S OFTEN CHOCOLATE	**$600**	WHAT IS
ONE VARIATION OF THIS COOKIE IS THE DOUBLE STUF, WITH TWICE THE CREME FILLING OF THE ORIGINAL	**$800**	WHAT IS
SEA CAPTAIN HANSON GREGORY & THE PENNSYLVANIA DUTCH ARE BOTH CREDITED WITH PUTTING THE HOLE IN THIS TREAT	**$1000**	WHAT IS

DOUBLE JEOPARDY!

JUST DESSERTS

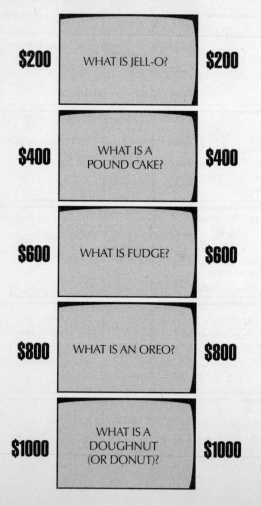

$200 — WHAT IS JELL-O? — $200

$400 — WHAT IS A POUND CAKE? — $400

$600 — WHAT IS FUDGE? — $600

$800 — WHAT IS AN OREO? — $800

$1000 — WHAT IS A DOUGHNUT (OR DONUT)? — $1000

DOUBLE JEOPARDY!

FILMS OF THE '50s

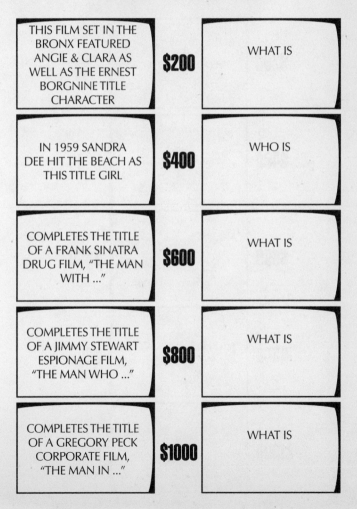

THIS FILM SET IN THE BRONX FEATURED ANGIE & CLARA AS WELL AS THE ERNEST BORGNINE TITLE CHARACTER	**$200**	WHAT IS
IN 1959 SANDRA DEE HIT THE BEACH AS THIS TITLE GIRL	**$400**	WHO IS
COMPLETES THE TITLE OF A FRANK SINATRA DRUG FILM, "THE MAN WITH ..."	**$600**	WHAT IS
COMPLETES THE TITLE OF A JIMMY STEWART ESPIONAGE FILM, "THE MAN WHO ..."	**$800**	WHAT IS
COMPLETES THE TITLE OF A GREGORY PECK CORPORATE FILM, "THE MAN IN ..."	**$1000**	WHAT IS

DOUBLE JEOPARDY!

FILMS OF THE '50s

$200	WHAT IS "MARTY"?	**$200**
$400	WHO IS GIDGET?	**$400**
$600	WHAT IS "THE GOLDEN ARM"?	**$600**
$800	WHAT IS "KNEW TOO MUCH"?	**$800**
$1000	WHAT IS "THE GRAY FLANNEL SUIT"?	**$1000**

DOUBLE JEOPARDY!

WORLD CAPITALS

DURING THE MIDDLE AGES, THIS CAPITAL WAS MOSTLY CONFINED TO STADSHOLMEN & RIDDARHOLMEN ISLANDS	**$200**	WHAT IS
ALEXANDER NEVSKY CATHEDRAL IN THE CENTER OF THIS BULGARIAN CITY CELEBRATES ITS LIBERATION FROM THE TURKS	**$400**	WHAT IS
IN THIS CAPITAL, YOU CAN WATCH THE SUN TURN THE TAGUS' ESTUARY INTO MAR DE PALHA, THE SEA OF STRAW	**$600**	WHAT IS
DIPLOMATS LIVE IN THE CHANAKYAPURI SECTION OF THIS CAPITAL DESIGNED BY EDWIN LUTYENS & HERBERT BAKER	**$800**	WHAT IS
FROM 1936 TO 1961 THIS CARIBBEAN CAPITAL WAS KNOWN AS CIUDAD TRUJILLO IN HONOR OF DICTATOR RAFAEL TRUJILLO	**$1000**	WHAT IS

DOUBLE JEOPARDY!

WORLD CAPITALS

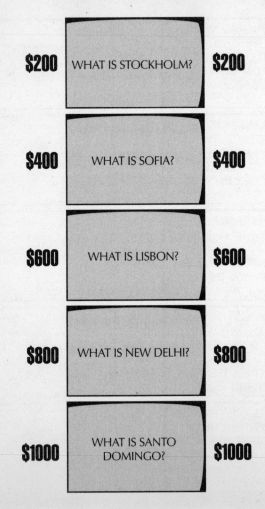

$200   WHAT IS STOCKHOLM? $200

$400   WHAT IS SOFIA? $400

$600   WHAT IS LISBON? $600

$800   WHAT IS NEW DELHI? $800

$1000   WHAT IS SANTO DOMINGO? $1000

DOUBLE JEOPARDY!

AMERICAN REVOLUTIONARIES

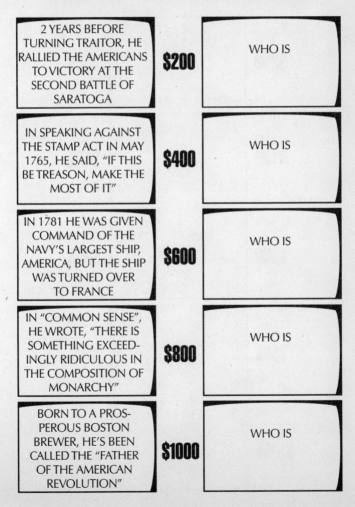

Clue	Value	Response
2 YEARS BEFORE TURNING TRAITOR, HE RALLIED THE AMERICANS TO VICTORY AT THE SECOND BATTLE OF SARATOGA	$200	WHO IS
IN SPEAKING AGAINST THE STAMP ACT IN MAY 1765, HE SAID, "IF THIS BE TREASON, MAKE THE MOST OF IT"	$400	WHO IS
IN 1781 HE WAS GIVEN COMMAND OF THE NAVY'S LARGEST SHIP, AMERICA, BUT THE SHIP WAS TURNED OVER TO FRANCE	$600	WHO IS
IN "COMMON SENSE", HE WROTE, "THERE IS SOMETHING EXCEEDINGLY RIDICULOUS IN THE COMPOSITION OF MONARCHY"	$800	WHO IS
BORN TO A PROSPEROUS BOSTON BREWER, HE'S BEEN CALLED THE "FATHER OF THE AMERICAN REVOLUTION"	$1000	WHO IS

DOUBLE JEOPARDY!

AMERICAN REVOLUTIONARIES

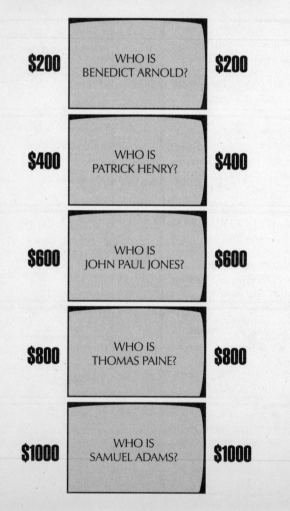

$200 · WHO IS BENEDICT ARNOLD? · $200

$400 · WHO IS PATRICK HENRY? · $400

$600 · WHO IS JOHN PAUL JONES? · $600

$800 · WHO IS THOMAS PAINE? · $800

$1000 · WHO IS SAMUEL ADAMS? · $1000

DOUBLE JEOPARDY!

BEFORE & AFTER

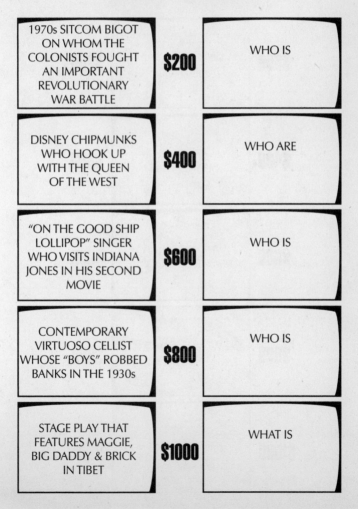

1970s SITCOM BIGOT ON WHOM THE COLONISTS FOUGHT AN IMPORTANT REVOLUTIONARY WAR BATTLE	$200	WHO IS
DISNEY CHIPMUNKS WHO HOOK UP WITH THE QUEEN OF THE WEST	$400	WHO ARE
"ON THE GOOD SHIP LOLLIPOP" SINGER WHO VISITS INDIANA JONES IN HIS SECOND MOVIE	$600	WHO IS
CONTEMPORARY VIRTUOSO CELLIST WHOSE "BOYS" ROBBED BANKS IN THE 1930s	$800	WHO IS
STAGE PLAY THAT FEATURES MAGGIE, BIG DADDY & BRICK IN TIBET	$1000	WHAT IS

DOUBLE JEOPARDY!

BEFORE & AFTER

$200 — WHO IS ARCHIE BUNKER HILL? — **$200**

$400 — WHO ARE CHIP & DALE EVANS? — **$400**

$600 — WHO IS SHIRLEY TEMPLE OF DOOM? — **$600**

$800 — WHO IS YO-YO MA BARKER? — **$800**

$1000 — WHAT IS "CAT ON A HOT TIN ROOF OF THE WORLD"? — **$1000**

FINAL JEOPARDY!

SPORTS

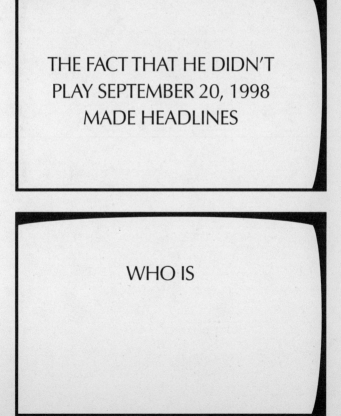

THE FACT THAT HE DIDN'T
PLAY SEPTEMBER 20, 1998
MADE HEADLINES

WHO IS

FINAL JEOPARDY!

SPORTS

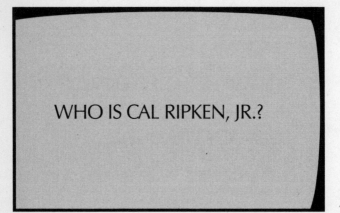

WHO IS CAL RIPKEN, JR.?